Citizen Soldier

From Sevastopol Street to Soloheadbeg:
Séumas Robinson and the Irish Revolution

Daniel Jack

HERITAGE FUND
Supported by
THE NATIONAL LOTTERY HERITAGE FUND

Connolly Publications
at Áras Uí Chonghaile

James Connolly was a man of remarkable ideas and a prolific writer. Many of his published works are recognised as timeless in both a social and political sense. Our readers' library provides an opportunity for visitors to engage with Connolly's writings, and as Áras Uí Chonghaile continues to evolve, we are thrilled to announce the establishment of Connolly Publications at Áras Uí Chonghaile. This new, dynamic and exciting publishing arm, will offer those inspired by the writings of James Connolly to follow in his footsteps, have their work published and made available to the wider public. We seek to uncover the talent of local people, provide a unique platform to showcase hidden history and explore contemporary political ideals.

Connolly Publications at Áras Uí Chonghaile are delighted to launch our first project in partnership with local author Daniel Jack.

Comandant General Séumas Robinson pictured in 1922.
At the time he was in command of the 2nd Southern
Division IRA.

Dedication

It is only right and fitting that I dedicate this work to the Robinson Family and their descendants near and far, known and unknown. What a fascinating journey I have had exploring our origins and discovering the 'quare mix' that has made us who we are. A special mention has to be given to my grandfather, Alex Robinson, a rebel in his own right who gave me a love for Ireland, her people and an interest in her history, particularly our own connections. Hopefully through this work I have been 'Faithful.'

Acknowledgements

Plenty of people have offered me help, encouragement, support and inspiration along the way. To them all, I am truly grateful. I have to give special mention to a few individuals. Firstly, Jim McVeigh, who has had many a discussion with me on this topic and encouraged me to persevere and do something with all my research; without him, this work would never have been completed. Liam Walsh, a proud Tipperary man, who used his local contacts and knowledge to enrich my research in its early stages and again of late, I am truly grateful and forever indebted to him for his efforts. A special mention must also be given to Kathleen Allis Cleary and Úna Crowe for guiding me around South Tipperary and giving a sense of place that no research could ever yield. I must also say thanks to Nora Shanahan for her kindness and hospitality. To the staff of the many libraries, archives and repositories who provided me with help and assistance. To Isabelle Rancourt, a Robinson descendant of the Irish Diaspora, who rekindled my interest in exploring the Robinson family lineage. My deepest gratitude is also given to Denis and Aidan, without their expertise and patience, this work would never have gone to print! I would also like to thank Seán Murray for contributing the Foreword, and to Clonard Residents Association for having faith in me to deliver this work as part of the 'Clonard Remembers – Is Cuimhin Linn' project. The National Lottery Heritage Fund must be thanked for their investment which gave us a platform to explore and share our local history and heritage. A special thanks must be extended to Lorraine Robinson (no relation!) at The National Lottery Heritage Fund for all her support and guidance throughout the lifespan of the grant. An exciting development that also emerged is the partnership with Connolly Publications at Áras Uí Chonghaile. It is a great privilege to have their support, and I am honoured that this book will be the first of many publications under their tutelage. Gerry Adams TD provided valuable insight, guidance and encouragement regarding publishing. Through him I received some very welcome suggestions in reference to the work, which, hopefully, have enhanced it. I will also be forever appreciative and indebted to Dimphne Brennan, daughter of Séumas Robinson, and also his son-in-law Joe MacAnthony, along with the wider family circle, who were all gracious enough to meet on a number of occasions and share memories, offer insights and information. They provided a personal connection that no amount of research from books or manuscripts could ever unfold. A gratitude of thanks, must also be extended to Conor Lenihan for making this priceless connection in the first instance. Finally, I would like to thank my family, especially my wife Eileen for all her help, support and proof reading!

FOREWORD

Daniel, in publishing this work, makes a valuable and essential contribution to the narrative around the development of militant Republicanism from the start of the last century. His contribution is also timely, as we are in the midst of the 'Decade of Centenaries' and reflect back upon the 100th anniversary of the genesis of the War of Independence and the revolutionary actions of Volunteers like Séumas Robinson as manifested in the Soloheadbeg Ambush.

In my own area of Clonard in West Belfast, we have a number of groups within the local community who have done great work over the years looking at the historical heritage of the area. Daniel has played a key role in that work by carrying out essential research related to our cherished local narrative. We have a rich heritage in this little part of Belfast that spans the political, social and economic spheres.

As part of the 'Clonard Remembers – Is Cuimhin Linn' project, which has been kindly supported by The National Lottery Heritage Fund, we organised a series of successful commemorative events examining August 1969 and the lasting impact that period has had on our community and indeed on wider society.

The roots of the conflict that erupted in 1969 can be traced back to the period of political change that occurred as a consequence of the years incorporating the Irish Revolution and the subsequent partition imposed upon the island. These were pivotal times and, in many senses, can be seen as the crucible of modern Ireland, and the subject of this work, Séumas Robinson, played a central role in that period. This study looks at the extraordinary journey that took him from Sevastopol Street, here in the Greater Clonard area, to participation in the 1916 Easter Rising, a leadership role in the Soloheadbeg Ambush and other militant actions through to his membership of the Second Dáil and tragically to involvement in the Irish Civil War.

Daniel is rightfully proud of his family links to Séumas Robinson and the fact that he lived in the Clonard area for part of his life. However, in capturing the contribution of Robinson and his influence in the Irish Revolution, he highlights the key role of individuals as leaders of the Republican Movement. Highly motivated and committed men and women, they provided the vision, dynamic and direction so essential to the prosecution of a bloody, brutal and sustained conflict, the consequences of which still reverberate for Irish people today.

I hope that this is the first of many of such contributions to the recording of our history, and we hope to continue the work of 'Clonard Remembers – Is Cuimhin Linn' into the future to examine other events that have influenced and shaped us as a community. It is imperative that we contribute to the writing and recording of our own history and interweave it within the wider chronicle of key events which have shaped the past and continues to influence our country's journey.

Seán Murray
Chairperson, Clonard Residents Association

Notes on Sources

Readers will notice that this work does not contain in text citations. This is due to a number of factors. Largely, this present work began as a short local history booklet but expanded into something more in-depth. It was never intended to be an academic endeavour; instead, its purpose was to share the story of Séumas Robinson in an accessible format. Throughout the text I have strived to identity and attribute quotes to authors and Witnesses. In spite of this lack of formal references I have, nevertheless, utilised various sources and here I wish to outline some.

Upon commencing my original research into Séumas Robinson I found that there were scant references to him dotted throughout academic texts. He received a small mention here and there and was quite often relegated to footnotes or reference pages. Therefore, my use of academic texts was limited mainly to guidance around context and chronology. Of late there has been more work carried out into specific aspects of the period under examination which has a particular relevancy, including Gerard Noonan's work on Republicans in Britain, Denis Marnane's in-depth history of the Third Tipperary Brigade and John Reynolds's study of the RIC in Tipperary.

Memoirs from IRA veterans and books written by contemporaries such as Ernie O'Malley, Desmond Ryan and Florence O'Donoghue provided valuable insight. It would be remiss not to mention Dan Breen's *My Fight for Irish Freedom*, always a lively and entertaining read despite its hyperbole.

In the first instance my research centred upon Robinson's Witness Statement to the Bureau of Military History. The files were not yet open to the public, and I relied upon a copy that was part of the Frank Gallagher papers housed in the National Library of Ireland. I also utilised documents kept in UCD archives such as Ernie O'Malley's papers, many of which are now being published, and those of Con Moloney. I also travelled to the British Public Record Office in Kew and accessed a considerable quantity of British War Office and Colonial Office files, uncovering lots of interesting papers regarding Robinson, his imprisonment after 1916 and intelligence reports into his later activities.

The depth of this current work was made possible by the opening of the Military History Bureau Files and Military Pension Applications. Both are rich sources of information but have to be read with a number of factors in mind, including the timespan between when they were written and the events they were recording. The Irish Civil War also looms large over many of the accounts as does other human factors such as personalities, people overplaying their roles, antagonisms and animosities. Many surviving key players didn't leave accounts either thus leaving some vital gaps. The various Witness Statements have most definitely accentuated my previous research and provided an additional layer of enrichment.

I sincerely hope that this work contributes to the wider understanding of the period, identifies Séumas Robinson as a crucial protagonist and integrates him firmly back into the historical narrative.

NB: Robinson spelt his forename as Séumas and for consistency I have used this spelling throughout this work. I have changed the spelling in quotes from others who have used Séamus to avoid any confusion.

INTRODUCTION

In my mind there lurks...a conception (deception?), a perception, an inception that the following agglomeration of reminiscences will be "My Last Will and Testament."

Séumas Robinson

I am absolutely delighted to have finally produced something on the life of Séumas Robinson for public consumption. This endeavour has turned into my magnus opus! While it is not intended to be an in-depth history of Séumas Robinson and the period of the Irish Revolution, it is, nevertheless, in part, intended to be his story. His thoughts, his words, his deeds, his feelings and his opinions have shaped this work. It has always been my aim to do something more thorough, but alas life has always gotten in the way. I keenly felt that it was important to produce something on his life as we mark the 'Decade of Centenaries' including the 100-year anniversary of the Soloheadbeg Ambush, which Robinson commanded and is widely regarded as the first shots fired in the Irish War for Independence, and to highlight the connection between a little district in Belfast and one of the pivotal moments in modern Irish history.

The foundations of this work began as my MA dissertation almost 20 years ago but it has a longer gestation through my grandfather, Alex Robinson. He always spoke of a relative who had taken part in the Easter Rising and subsequently led the South Tipperary Brigade of the Irish Republican Army (IRA) during the period spanning 1917-1923. Indeed, my grandfather remembered as a young child meeting this relative. His abiding memory was of a man with a black leather travelling bag staying in their home situated in the Clonard area. During my research I was later to find out that this bag – such a vivid memory from my grandfather's childhood – was in fact, synonymous with Séumas Robinson and was often associated with him by his comrades in their recollections of the period. This meeting with my grandfather most likely occurred around October 1918 after Séumas Robinson was released from Crumlin Road Gaol, where he had served a short sentence for drilling Volunteers in South Tipperary. During his time in 'The Crum' there had been a 'mutiny' by the Republican prisoners over conditions and political status. By all accounts, they went through a turbulent time. Séumas Robinson played a central role in that episode and he was remembered by his comrades from prison as a steely and determined fighter.

As someone with an acute interest in Irish history, this family connection had always fascinated me, and as I was looking for an original subject matter for my thesis a study of Séumas Robinson and the role that he played during the Irish Revolution seemed to fit the bill. No other work has specifically focused on Robinson. This I found quite surprising as he seemed to be a person who played such a crucial part in the events of that period.

Further fuel was added to my interest in Robinson after reading Ernie O'Malley's experiences in the Third Tipperary Brigade area during the War for Independence. In the first instalment of his memoirs, *On Another Man's Wound*, he describes his exploits with the two principal IRA officers, Seán Treacy and Séumas Robinson. He described Robinson as being 'pudgey and took short steps, which were hard on my long stride. Brown eyes helped a grin when he played on words; he liked to pun even to the limit of our groans. He had a slight clipping speech that came from Belfast, stout stubborn under lip and sparse hair on a high round forehead.'

The organisation of the IRA during this period is regarded by historians as being highly parochial, with the leadership coming from within the locality. As noted by the academic Peter Hart, 'Companies were usually formed on local initiative by self-nominated organisers: entrepreneurs who could rely on their crowd to back them up.' Therefore, how did a man who hailed originally from a northern industrial city, and who was cited to be a left-leaning 'Social Republican,' become the Brigadier of the mainly rural and somewhat conservative South Tipperary IRA?

On closer examination, Séumas Robinson and his contribution to the Irish Revolution is a fascinating topic. His obituary in the *Irish Press* described him as 'the ideal Citizen Soldier. He came to the fight for Irish Freedom via Belfast and Glasgow because he realised that such a step was necessary.'

Through his writings, Séumas Robinson emerges as a man fully aware of who he was, what he had done and, perhaps more importantly, why he had done it. He was a man of obvious intellect with a good education, both of which were linked to a vast astuteness that trusted upon strong instinct and common-sense. His conscience was very much at ease with the part that he played during a very turbulent period in Irish history. Orders that he gave are widely regarded as kick-starting the War for Independence at Soloheadbeg. The move towards armed struggle was subsequently reinforced at Knocklong Station, with Robinson and his comrades carrying out the daring rescue of Seán Hogan as he was being transported to Cork Gaol and an almost certain rendezvous with a hangman's noose.

Robinson was a complex character with many and varied influences which bore upon him. He was a man of independent thought and action yet, in many senses, he comes across as being humble, quiet and unassuming. Perhaps these traits are contributing factors towards his role becoming a footnote in the pages of history books. Indeed, Séumas Robinson was personally very hurt by the way in which he felt some former comrades in arms from Tipperary subsequently treated him, helping to relegate his commanding role in favour of themselves or others.

When in Tipperary, Robinson's staunchest comrade was Brigade Vice-Commandant Seán Treacy. These two men proved to be a lethal combination, a virtual Molotov cocktail that would ignite South Tipperary, and undeniably Ireland, into militant action. Treacy greatly admired Séumas Robinson and on many an occasion deferred to his judgement in relation to military matters, strategy and tactics. This in part stemmed from the fact that Robinson had fought in the Easter Rising, but there was also mutual respect and a close bond of comradeship. It is often stated that guerrillas develop such a close relationship. They have a shared experience that is often one forged by great hardship, deprivation and constantly fraught with danger; certainly, that was the case for active IRA personnel in South Tipperary during the period under examination.

Robinson, an outsider in Tipperary, could be extremely ruthless in the actions he promulgated but equally he could display great humanity and issued orders that tried to protect civilians. He was acutely aware of the need for the people's support. To drive a wedge between the IRA and the civilian population, the British began to use the tactic of reprisal, destroying homes and livelihoods. Robinson, with no local ties, pushed ahead with the campaign. This was to become a point of contention with some of the Tipperary men who sought to be more cautious. It became apparent that some officers like Frank Drohan and, indeed the man who brought Robinson to Tipperary in the first instance, Éamon Ó Duibhir tried to apply the brakes on the pace of the war effort due to the effect of the British reprisal policy in the locality.

The fact that Robinson had Seán Treacy on his side was of enormous benefit. Treacy proved to be that insider. He provided the local touch; he was well-known and respected in the command area and surrounding districts, vital in the close, clannish world of South Tipperary. They were the dynamic behind the war effort. When Treacy was killed in action during a gun battle in Dublin, it came as an extremely bitter blow for Robinson, and he found it difficult to exert full command in the area. Many veterans, upon reflection, felt that if Robinson was listened to more then Tipperary would have had less to lament in terms of missed opportunities.

In my examination of Séumas Robinson, he comes across as a very devout man, not only with his Republican ideology but also in terms of his religious beliefs. At one time he even contemplated taking Holy Orders and entered a seminary in Scotland but he received another calling in life that would lead him on a very different path. When the fight for Irish Freedom was looming, Robinson engaged the Abbott and provided a moral and theological argument that he should participate in the liberation of his Country. As a reward for his sincerity and conviction, Séumas Robinson received special dispensation by his superior to leave his vocation. Often described as a 'gentlemanly man,' many have found it difficult to reconcile the Séumas Robinson described by Tim Pat Coogan as a 'virtual warlord' with the kind, meek, gentle, humorous and affable man who went out of his way to do right by people.

Séumas Robinson was also a clear, logical, analytical and astutely clinical thinker. He possessed a military mind, advocating guerrilla warfare and even a military campaign in England to strike at the enemy on their own territory. He felt that this latter move would impact greater than any fighting that took place in Ireland. He also felt that each IRA Battalion should have went out every day with the express purpose of killing at least one member of the Crown Forces, thus sapping their morale and making the country ungovernable. He believed that the IRA needed to be a 'Ghostly Army of Sharpshooters' that could attack their targets and seamlessly melt back into their environment. He drew these conclusions from his own experiences during the 1916 Easter Rising which, he believed, showed the futility of having a stand-up fight against superior odds. However, with the outbreak of the Irish Civil War, Robinson logically thought that the IRA should have changed tactics and had a decisive battle with the Free State forces in Dublin, 'to cut the cancer before it spread' and carry out a pre-emptive strike while their enemy was in a weak position.

His initial observations regarding the Free State Army was that it was disorganised, poorly trained and ill-equipped. He thought the IRA should have exploited this weakness and went on the offensive. Perhaps, if Robinson's counsel had been heeded, the outcome of the Civil War could have been very different. A lightning strike would have circumvented the bitter conflict that ensued and would have been a lot kinder to the country. Robinson argued with the other IRA leaders over the prevailing tactics and he felt so strongly about the merits of his position that he was prepared to resign his commission. Liam Lynch, the then IRA Chief of Staff, begged him to remain in his command at such a critical juncture.

The result of the Civil War was military defeat for Republicans. IRA personnel were ordered to dump arms. The future looked bleak, the years of 'Glorious Unity' had been well and truly shattered. Yet, Republicans were still a force with which to be reckoned. Despite all the executions, jailing and internment, they won 44 seats in the Free State elections in 1923. Under the banner of Sinn Féin, the wider Movement adhered to abstentionism. Éamon de Valera felt that this policy would keep them in the political wilderness, and if the Oath of Allegiance to

17

the British Crown could be circumvented, then Republicans should take their seats and become the opposition in the Free State Dáil. This debate caused another schism within the ranks of Republicanism and de Valera formed Fianna Fáil in 1926 with the express aim of undermining and eventually destroying the detested Treaty from within. Many serving and former IRA Officers and Volunteers consented to this new departure. Fianna Fáil's subtitle was 'The Republican Party' and with the support of the IRA they came to power in 1932. However, de Valera soon turned on his erstwhile comrades and began to imprison and eventually execute IRA activists.

Included within the founding members of Fianna Fáil was Séumas Robinson. He had made the transition from being a 'warlord' to a 'slightly constitutional' politician. Robinson was elected a Senator in 1928 but he never really seemed fully comfortable with that role and resigned his seat early. Séumas Robinson was a sincere and honest man and perhaps he was not suited for the cut and thrust of the political world.

After politics Robinson's time was consumed with working in trusted positions within the civil service, first with the Military Service Pensions Board, then the Bureau of Military History and finally the Military Registration Board. He worked tirelessly, helping people with their pension claims, always going that extra mile to ensure that former comrades received what they deserved from the State for their contribution during the Campaign for Independence.

As previously alluded to, the core sources for this work are a series of autobiographical 'Witness Statements' compiled by Robinson for the Irish Military History Bureau. This body was founded in 1947 to assemble and coordinate material to form the basis of the history of the Independence Movement from the formation of the Irish Volunteers on 25 November 1913 to the

Truce of 11 July 1921. Michael Mc Dunphy was its director, Colonel Dan Bryan, John Mc Coy, Major Florence O'Donoghue and Séumas Robinson were its members, and it had an advisory committee of a number of distinguished historians and academics.

Robinson acknowledged that his memoir was a retrospective look at the period. Most of the Statements for the Bureau were compiled more than 30 years after the events. They also need to be viewed through the lens of the Civil War. Robinson was acutely aware of all this and he wrote in his own Statement that 'Those of us involved in our recent history were, and are still, like the storied man in the forest who could not see the wood for the trees.'

The pace of events during the struggle dictated that most militant Republicans simply got on with the task in front of them. 'We were so intimately and urgently wrapped up in vital and mortal detail that we had no time or opportunity whatever about our inclination, "to stand and stare" or [in the Belfast vernacular] to be "a chiel among ye takin' notes" or to be bothered or distracted by anything outside our immediate ken.'

Séumas Robinson's memoir is at times quite revealing and is an invaluable source in helping to understand the events of the Irish Revolution. He articulated that the IRA was a localised organisation belonging to a national movement. 'Each responsible officer had to have, of course, his own bird's eye view of his own campaign and immediate tactics, but what happened to the other trees in the forest were not his concern...' This could help to explain the geographical variance of IRA activity. Peter Hart, looking at the geography of revolution in Ireland, observed that Commands in Cork under Volunteer Officers such as Liam Lynch, Tom Barry and Sean Moylan accounted for 39.1% of recorded incidents for the period 1917-1923 while Tipperary was responsible for 27.5%. Therefore, it was because of men like these and Séumas Robinson that the guerrilla war was fought. It was not down to a grand plan that emanated from General Headquarters but rather was forged in the field by individual commands that took the initiative and delivered.

Areas with responsible, motivated and resourceful officers proved to be the most industrious. And perhaps, if it had not been for IRA leaders like Robinson who ordered and encouraged his command to engage the British Forces (often without GHQ permission), then the War for Independence may never have happened. This episode in Irish history has plenty of unsung heroes; often the role of such people has been forgotten and replaced by the big, famous, charismatic figures.

The period of the revolution was to have a dramatic and lasting effect upon Robinson. There was a hidden cost to the period, one that is not often spoken about. It took a toll on lots of people including Robinson whose physical health was affected. Seán Hogan, a staunch comrade of Robinson, would have mental health struggles that would plague him the rest of his days. He eventually came to live with the Robinson family in Dublin for a period, and Séumas's daughter remembered that when 'Uncle Seán' stayed, he confined himself to his room.

Robinson's life and career were coloured by past events and experiences. He believed that 'those of our generation who took, or "had thrust upon them" some responsibility during the campaigns for Independence from 1916 – 1923 should write their memoirs for the benefit of future generations. Everyone's story is unique and will almost certainly be of interest to a whole section of the community.'

Yet, he felt that there was a danger in this too. He did not want his own memoir to be treated as a matter of fact history but rather to be 'regarded as a monologue on the mental meanderings of a babe in the woods.' Furthermore 'I am humble enough to realise that despite all my efforts to see things correctly I may be objectively wrong.'

What might be perceived as a 'fact' may be 'a lie and a half… the whole truth can't be presented – only an angel can record the truth absolute. History can lie like a trooper through suppressions, by wrongful juxta-positioning, by wilfully drawing wrong or misleading conclusions, by over emphasis or understatement, by drawing "red herrings," by "throwing monkey wrenches" and by crass ignorance but mostly by paucity of judgement, lack of clarity or want of thought.'

Robinson came to these conclusions through his own experiences. After the struggle, many IRA veterans published memoirs, and their stories were celebrated as heroic contributions in the fight for freedom. Commemorations were held for fallen comrades or to mark significant events. In Tipperary the role played by Séumas Robinson was marginalised; he was forgotten, or worse, he was ignored, why? His sister-in-law Kathleen Kincaid asked the question, 'Surely it is not because Séumas Robinson hails from the same part of Ireland as Seán an Daoimhis, Roger Casement, Jemmy Hope, Henry Joy Mc Cracken, Willie Orr, General Monroe, Betsy Grey, Joe Mc Kelvey and many others…' Locals, such as Dan Breen, were elevated in Tipperary, and many seemed 'ashamed to acknowledge Séumas Robinson as the man solely responsible for starting the "racket" at Soloheadbeg and leading South Tipperary all through the long fighting. That Séumas Robinson was the originating and directing brain behind the fight in South Tipperary.' Books and articles on the period still neglect his commanding role even though some historians have begun to use his 'Statements' as a source.

Séumas Robinson died on 8 December 1961 and was buried at Glasnevin Cemetery. According to a press report:

> …full military honours were rendered at the funeral of Commandant General Séumas Robinson, the veteran IRA leader, which took place yesterday morning from the Church of the Three Patrons, Rathgar. Amongst the very large attendance was the President, Mr de Valera; the Taoiseach, Mr Lemass, and members of the Government and both Houses of the Oireachtas. A guard of honour drawn from the 2nd Motor Squadron escorted the remains to the cemetery where a firing party rendered honours. Buglers from the No. 1 Army Band, under Commandant J. Doherty, sounded the last post as the coffin, draped with the tricolour, was lowered to the grave. Mr. Oscar Traynor, the former Minister for Justice, in an oration, said that no writer of the history of Ireland's latest fight for freedom could ignore the deeds for which Séumas Robinson was responsible or the valour with which they were carried out. "It can be truly said that no member of the Irish Republican Army, whether Officer or Volunteer, could have exceeded the service given by him. He not only planned the actions which took place under his command but he insisted on personally seeing them carried out."

Many contributions to the campaign for Irish Independence in the period spanning 1916 -23 are well known; here is that of Séumas Robinson.

CHAPTER ONE

THE FAITH THAT IS IN ME

Born and bred in Belfast and Glasgow: 1890 - 1916

In his 'Witness Statements' Séumas Robinson went to great lengths to help the reader understand why he had become a militant Irish Republican, to account for 'the faith that is in me.' The formation of a revolutionary is a complex process. What influences and motivations help convert a 'normal Irish Catholic Nationalist boy' into a dedicated militant Republican? Séumas Robinson possessed deeply held religious beliefs that often came into conflict with his 'Fenian Ideal.' Nevertheless, he did develop a political ideology that went as deep as his religious convictions. He came to this avenue through a mixture of family and societal influences. His education and membership of organisations that were deemed virtual 'spawning beds' for revolutionaries, all within the context of a gradual militarisation of Irish society, help explain why Robinson became, in his words a 'militant separatist' and took the path of revolutionary armed struggle:

> We are told that Dean Swift cursed the day that he was born. He must have been a very precocious day-old chick! Now it was God's will that I should not be born a precocious little chicken...nor to become a precocious youth – but just a normal Irish Catholic Nationalist boy. I hope that boy is still father to the man.

Séumas Robinson's story begins in a spot that is now well-known. If you travel up the Falls Road from Belfast City Centre, one of the most prominent and striking features is a wall mural dedicated to local IRA hunger strikers. The centre piece of this art work is an iconic image of Bobby Sands. Day and daily, a multitude of tourists visit Belfast to see a city in transition. Inevitably, they also seek to get a glimpse into the recent conflict. These visitors can be seen regularly posing in front of this mural, a captured image of their trip for posterity. Throughout key moments of the Peace Process, Gerry Adams and Martin Mc Guinness along with other members of Sinn Féin were interviewed by the media using the image as a backdrop. This mural is located on the gable wall of McKelvey House, a Sinn Féin office which is named after legendary Belfast IRA figure Joe Mc Kelvey who was executed by the Free State Provisional Government on 8 December 1922 during the Irish Civil War. The caption on the mural proclaims that 'Everyone Republican or Otherwise Has His/Her Own Part to Play,' so it is perhaps fitting that all these Republican connections converge here in Sevastopol Street as Séumas Robinson, who played a heroic and central role during the struggle for freedom from 1916 – 1923, was born here at number 22 on 6 January 1890. He was the third child for James Robinson and his wife Sarah (neé Black), both of whom were, interestingly, born in France. A plaque has now been erected in the street to mark Robinson's historical link to the locality.

The Falls Road was quite different then: cobble-stoned streets, horses and carts, masses of mill workers passing wearily along the terraced house lined streets. Belfast was the manufacturing hub of Ireland. Industries such as shipbuilding, linen and rope works all helped transform it from a small market town and port into one of the Victorian era's great industrial cities, generating huge wealth for some in the process.

James Connolly, trade union organiser and subsequent revolutionary leader, described a profit-grinding capitalist class existent in Belfast, who all became abundantly wealthy. They built grandiose houses and generally enjoyed the privileges that came with having such a hefty purse. However, the people living in the working-class areas - the cannon fodder for the industrial revolution - did not benefit from the fruits of their labour. Their experience was the grim face on the flip side of Belfast's industrialisation.

Survival was a hard-fought battle. Living in cramped and squalid conditions, diseases such as tuberculosis were rampant; indeed, Séumas's brother George succumbed to one of these poverty-related illnesses and died in 1894 at the tender age of six. Men, women and children had to work in appallingly cruel conditions just to etch out a meagre existence. The unskilled nature of much of the work meant that wages were low. People were often grateful that they were employed in the first instance, and so workers rarely organised to challenge their employers over pay and conditions.

The sectarian division of the city also exacerbated this situation. In the years during and after the Great Hunger in the 1840s and 1850s, a mass exodus of people from rural areas increased the population of Belfast, importing many of the stresses, strains and animosities that were prevalent in the countryside into the once liberal and enlightened city. The fallout and consequences of the 1798 Rebellion cast a long shadow over Belfast which was once lauded as the 'Athens of the North.' The birthplace of Irish Republicanism and the Society of United Irishmen was to become a cauldron of seething sectarian passions that would periodically erupt into orgies of violence and destruction, often directed against the small and vulnerable Catholic population. In the city, people remained in tight, close knit communities. Kith and kin provided support and protection, helping to create single identity districts that are still a feature of the Belfast of today and are physically lineated by the so-called 'Peacelines.' An atmosphere of fear, suspicion and distrust was fostered in such an environment which sustained the divisions within the confines of the city.

It was into this humble and somewhat unpredictable setting that Séumas Robinson entered this world. His family soon moved to the newly built houses in the Clonard area, just a short distance away from their original home in Sevastopol Street. The centrepiece of this new district, *Clonard House,* was the former home of the Kennedy family who were synonymous with the Belfast linen industry. This neo-classical style house was taken over by the Catholic Redemptorist Order prior to the erection of Clonard Church and Monastery to help minister to the expanding Catholic population of the city. Today it is still in use and has been incorporated into a sheltered housing development.

Fr Paddy O'Donnell, in his brief history of Clonard Church and Monastery, recorded that a wide expanse of green land existed around *Clonard House* which was eventually bought and developed by RJ McConnell and Co.; 'the result was over 500 houses in 13 streets. The area was bounded by Cupar Street and the Springfield Road while in the south and east lay a row of mills, the Blackstaff, Milford's, Ross's, Clonard Print Works and Greaves.' The houses were a mixture between the working-class dwellings in the two-up two-down model and the more middle-class parlour houses with attics.

The new Catholic district straddled the Protestant Shankill area and due to this close proximity was to become a sectarian flash point, or in today's parlance an interface. Séumas Robinson recalled that even in the relative quiet days of his boyhood around the Clonard area he 'became an expert stone thrower in our own special "No Man's Land" between the Protestant and

Catholic communities, which was the field at the rear of Traver's factory on the Springfield Road.' The Clonard area would remain in the 'front-line' throughout the years. In July 1920, Séumas's cousin, Thomas Robinson, would be shot dead by British Military during disturbances on Kashmir Road. Homes, including those of remaining relatives of Robinson, would be destroyed during the outbreak of violence in August 1969. Robinson would grow up to detest any sort of prejudice or sectarianism due to his childhood experiences.

Family life in working class districts in Belfast was characterised by close relationships. The wider Robinson family mainly lived in adjacent streets around Clonard and the Springfield Road. Séumas Robinson described his own household as a normal Irish Catholic family. 'Our faults and failing as a family were many, but it was always a case of "Thus far thou shalt go and no further."'

Living in a working-class area so close to the Redemptorist religious community was bound to have a profound influence upon Robinson's spiritual and temporal convictions. He was a devout Catholic and yet he also experienced at first hand the poverty of Belfast's working classes, which in turn led him to the conclusion that Jesus was on the side of the marginalized, the oppressed and the poor and thus it was the incumbent duty of all Catholics to do likewise. He possessed a social conscience, which could be characterised as being akin to 'Liberation Theology,' socialistic in leaning and anti-imperialist in content. According to historian Conor Foley, Robinson's left wing orientated outlook would ensure that he was labelled as 'being close to the Reds.'

Governing his thoughts 'like other normal Catholic young people when a serious decision of judgement had to be made was the subject matter of the Hail Mary – "Now and at the hour of our death, Amen.'" Robinson wanted to put on record that Irish separatists were 'the normal, natural, (common) sensible people of Ireland' and not the bloodthirsty band of cutthroats, gunmen and criminals of British propaganda, and that they considered the consequences of their actions for both this life and the next.

Despite his personal devotion to faith and family, there was clearly a generational gap emerging in the Ireland at the turn of the twentieth century. Robinson reflected:

> My parents were ordinary typical Catholic nationalists of their day. Their sympathy lay with Parnell but could not take sides against the Bishops. They had become convinced that the British Empire had become invincible... 'It would be lovely if it could be done [ending British rule],' we were told, 'but your grandfathers failed and your great grandfathers failed, all better men than you could hope to be, and besides England has become much stronger and [is] just as ruthless.' I think it was Joe, my brother, who pointed out to me that we should be ashamed of my father's generation. They were the first generation of Irishmen not to have struck a blow for Ireland.

This cautious and constitutional political outlook was met with scorn by the youthful zeal and impatience of the new generation of Irish Republicans who were emerging. Therefore, in the political arena, the family influence on Séumas came in the form of his older brother Joe. Séumas recalled that 'Joe had always been determined to devote his life to the Fenian Ideal and did not want me actively engaged in the movement so that I could look after the old people at home while he would be carefree.'

Despite their parents' Home Rule tendencies, there was a physical force tradition in the family stretching back to 1798. It was not until Séumas was 20 years of age that he learned that 'my grandfather had been a Fenian and that was the reason my father and the younger members of his family were born in France. The grandfather had been able to get to France after '48 with the help of his Protestant employer who had great regard for him and his ability as an engineer.' Séumas's grandfather, James Robinson, was politically active and was involved in the Young Ireland Movement and the Reprieve Campaign for William Smith O'Brien. While in exile, it seems that James Robinson set up factory machinery all over north-eastern France and western Germany, helping to start German industry at the middle of the nineteenth century. He eventually returned to Ireland and settled in Belfast where he gained employment at Ross's Mill in what was to become the Clonard area. He is listed in the street directories from the 1870s period as living adjacent to the mill in Odessa Street and his occupation is recorded as 'Machine Master.'

James Robinson kept his Republican outlook and became a member of the secret oath-bound separatist organisation the Irish Republican Brotherhood (IRB). According to family tradition he swore to never shave again until Ireland was free. Apparently, he had a flowing white beard when he died in 1894.

Séumas Robinson attributed, in part, the lack of fighting spirit in his parents' generation stemmed from the power that the Catholic Church hierarchy wielded in the political life of the country. Notwithstanding his own personal devoutness, he still felt that:

> Irishmen who were anxious to shake-off foreign yoke were hampered (hamstrung as the Yanks would say) by the Jansenistic fulmination of so many of our religious mentors! These teachers taught us not to render to rapacious murdering Caesars what was their only due – the business

end of lethal weapons. Instead they encouraged Irishmen to join the British seizers' army and commanded us to voluntarily contribute to our and to other people's tribulation...

Events far away in South Africa demonstrated to the wider world that the British Army was not invincible, and Séumas Robinson recalled the impact that these events had on their thinking:

> As I have said, the arguments were all on our parents' side, until the Boer War. Heaven what thrills we got out of that great struggle. Bonfires in the streets on the news of a Boer victory, complete disbelief in Boer reverses. 'The Irish Boer Brigade,' how we wished we were old enough to be with them. Yet all these years and for many more the dark cloud of the Irish Bishops' attitude hung like a pall over every generous impulse to free our country.

The influence of the Church was powerful and impacted upon separatist sentiment and action. Robinson felt that the Bishops never gave any reason for condemning Irish separatists – 'they just condemned us.' His allegiance to the Catholic faith was never affected by the stance of the Bishops; he believed in the inherent righteousness of his temporal and spiritual beliefs. He expressed that:

> I am not bound to believe in its efficacy, nor am I always bound to accept as morally binding the application of any particular article or particle of the Church's teaching or discipline by any particular member of the clergy when such an interpretation is contrary to common sense or natural law and therefore not the universal teaching of the Church.

His acceptance of a higher power transcended the opinions or interpretations of mere mortal men.

The wind of change was blowing through Ireland and new people with different and radical notions on the relationship between Britain and Ireland were coming of age. One such person was Joe Robinson, who was to play a leading role in the revitalisation of the Republican Movement. He was the first lad to join the original Fianna Éireann in Belfast when Bulmer Hobson founded the organisation there in 1902. Many veteran Belfast Republicans mention Joe in their reminiscences of the period. Cathal O'Shannon remembers him as a Fianna officer while Liam Gaynor recalled that he was constantly smuggling weapons and explosives from Glasgow to Belfast. Séumas Robinson stated he knew his brother was 'an open militant Nationalist and was an admirer of the Fenians and didn't seem to be the least bit worried about excommunication: yet in those days he was an ardent Catholic.'

Like any other young person, education would have an immense impact on Robinson. He attended the Dominican Convent Schools, Falls Road, the De La Salle Brothers' school, Clonard and finally the Irish Christian Brothers school, St Mary's, Divis Street. The Christian Brothers have been identified as a particularly potent influence with a curriculum focused around 'Faith and Fatherland.' As well as teaching with an emphasis on the practical, they instilled in their pupils a strong view of an Irish-Ireland through the promotion of native history, language and sport. This promotion of all aspects of Gaelic culture ensured that those who were bright and patriotic were processed through the system with great skill and vigour. One observer, Dr Todd Andrews, noted that 'without the groundwork of the Christian Brothers' schooling, it is improbable that there would have been a 1916 Rising. The leadership of the IRA came from those who got their education from the Brothers.'

Séumas Robinson believed that education was vital to the life of any nation. His ideas on education were akin to those of

Pádraig Pearse. Referring to the education system in the Irish Free State, he observed:

> ...in our schools a good deal of thought, energy, patience and cane is expounded to impart practicable knowledge of the three Rs. No appeal is made to intellect – time is taken up with exams and only bright pupils succeed. [There is the] need for character forming instruction – pupils are not taught to think, to detect the differences between catch cries and full truth, fiction and fact, instead many of our people still join Freemasonic Imperialist armies to stamp out God given freedom the world over.

With established ideas of cultural distinctiveness, it is not surprising that notions of political distinctions became prevalent. Joost Augusteijn identified, 'In the environment of political struggle that had dominated Ireland since the 1880s, most Catholics grew up with the notion that Ireland was a separate nation and that England held that nation against its will...some people developed this notion into a willingness to fight.' The centenary celebrations of the 1798 rebellion brought this notion into perspective. Much literature was in circulation at the time extolling 'the deeds and noble stands made by the leaders.' School children vied with each other as to who knew the most about anyone or all the '98 leaders.

Séumas Robinson jokingly recalled that:

> My active service began in 1898 when, with more audacity than wit, I joined in a counter attack (made by an advance party of a Nationalist procession celebrating the '98 centenary) on a charging crowd of Orangemen. This Orange attack was launched from the fields where the new Celtic football grounds [Park Centre] now stands. I had not the least bit of fear – eight years of age. But as I grew older and

developed imagination so did physical fear grow in me, until now I am afraid of my wife.

Despite the novelty value of being present at a parade or even the sense of adventure or occasion, this incident highlights that even as a young lad of eight he had a growing awareness of his identity, especially in the sectarian charged atmosphere of the city. Belfast was the only place in Ireland where these celebrations were a major issue of contention, several nights of rioting followed, mainly on the Shankill Road, and so would have had a much more dramatic and lasting effect upon an impressionable young mind.

By the time that he was approaching his teenage years, Séumas Robinson had formed a solid sense of Irish identity. Hence, when 'a mass meeting of junior hurlers assembled at the Catholic Boy's Hall, Falls Road, on 22 June 1902 to form a junior league,' Joe and Séumas Robinson were present.

The mentor of this organisation was Bulmer Hobson, a young Quaker from Lisburn who had converted to Irish Republicanism. His papers, including the minutes books of Na Fianna are housed in the National Library, and they provide a keen sense of those early activities. Hobson along with Denis Mc McCullough and Seán Mac Diarmada worked tirelessly to revitalise separatist sentiment, particularly through the Irish Republican Brotherhood. Hobson hoped that this new boy's organisation, Na Fianna Éireann, would be a means of not only binding the boys together but also would be a mechanism of promoting the Gaelic revival among the young men of Belfast.

The Fianna was initially called the Red Branch Knights, reflecting the group's Ulster origins. However, it was soon renamed, and each club was to take the name of members of the mythical warrior band of the Fianna. The clubs were to play in competitions. Francis Joseph Bigger, a generous patron of everything Gaelic, commissioned the artist and craftsman Jack Morrow to make a shield of beaten copper as a prize. Classes in Irish history and language were an integral part of the organisation's activities. Hobson later recorded that 'The excitement was tremendous and I thought that here was something that we could mould into a strong force in the liberation of Ireland.'

Séumas Robinson recorded:

> My first definite contact with the national movement was when I joined the "Oscars" hurling club. This was one of the Fianna hurling clubs started in Belfast by Bulmer Hobson. There was a number of such clubs. I was too young to retain much detail of their activities or membership. The only activity, apart from hurling, which remains in my mind, is an attempt by Hobson to produce a play written by him on Wolfe Tone. I cannot remember if the play was ever produced. The members of these clubs I can remember the names of only few - my brother Joe, my cousin Willie Robinson, John and Michael Clarke, William Flanagan, and a boy named Ferris.

Although this was primarily a cultural organisation, it, nevertheless, possessed quite a militaristic character. As noted by David Fitzpatrick, a cult of discipline and training swept across Ireland and indeed Europe at the turn of the twentieth century. Society was becoming gradually more militarised, groups such as the Boy's Brigade and the Scouts were seen as 'the benign manifestation…of pseudo-military youth groups.' The Republican counterpart, Fianna Éireann, 'incalculated discipline and obedience, urging the boys to become strong and self-reliant, manly and independent.'

The Fianna initiative faltered due to a lack of funds; the boys came from poor working-class families and money was scarce. Nevertheless, it left a significant legacy, as some people who were associated with it later became active members of the IRA and the wider Republican Movement. Furthermore, it served as a precursor and blueprint to the national movement co-founded by Hobson and Countess Markievicz in 1909. Joe Robinson was instrumental in launching this rejuvenated Fianna. He became a full-time organiser and expanded the organisation across Ireland and into Irish communities throughout Britain. Members of the Fianna, including Joe Robinson, were to play a prominent role in the Howth gun running of 1914 and many were active participants in the 1916 Easter Rising.

The Robinson family, in keeping with the unfortunate Irish tradition of immigration, joined the Diaspora and moved to Glasgow in late 1903. There was increased economic activity in the city especially with the shipbuilding industry due to the imperial arms race between Britain and Germany; this rivalry would eventually culminate in the First World War. They resided at 10 Robson Street in the Govanhill area. Conditions in these working-class areas were just as dire as those in Belfast. Tragedy struck again, and Séumas's younger sister Mary died in 1903 shortly after the move to Scotland. She was just 10 years old.

Séumas continued his education at Marist Brothers schools and at Mount St Michael's College, Dumfries, where he passed the Scottish Intermediate exams. He gave up further study two years later, owing to eyestrain, and took up employment as an engineer with Montcalm and Moncouers. He contemplated taking a religious vocation and entered a seminary for a period. His Theological training emerges strongly in his writings. Military Orders would eclipse Holy Orders, and involvement in the struggle for Irish Independence would now preoccupy his thoughts and deeds.

In Glasgow the Irish community remained close knit, thus enhancing its distinct sense of identity. Séumas Robinson joined the Gaelic League, which promoted and encouraged the Gaelic revival. He developed a lifelong love of all aspects of Irish culture, particularly the language. Indeed, there was a tradition of Irish speaking in his family.

Developments in the Irish community in Glasgow closely mirrored those in Ireland. Separatist sentiment was growing and many organisations like the Dungannon Clubs and the IRB were active in promoting Republicanism. A branch of the Irish Volunteers was set up in Glasgow in December 1913. Séumas joined this organisation, becoming a member of 'A' Company of the Glasgow Battalion. Their meetings were held at various venues such as the Gaelic League Hall in London Street and a headquarters was established at a hall in Ann Street. Marches and drilling were a regular occurrence.

Despite his involvement with the Volunteers, Séumas did not become a member of the IRB until 1915. It was a decision that was not taken lightly, and it appears that he had a conscientious struggle about joining the secret, oath-bound revolutionary organisation. 'The amount of thought, theology and passionate longing that I went through and suffered to bring my conscience into line with the IRB ideal I cannot attempt to describe, but in the end, I was able to take the IRB manly oath in good faith.' Once inside the IRB, he was introduced to a world of espionage and conspiracy. Séumas was to have an uneasy relationship with 'The Organisation' and he never felt entirely comfortable with the cloak and dagger methods employed by the IRB.

After helping to re-establish Fianna Éireann, Joe, a prominent member of the IRB, set up a number of branches across Glasgow. From the outset he used the Fianna organisation in the secret quest to obtain arms and explosives. Many Glasgow

Republicans worked in the shipyards and munitions factories. Séumas Robinson recalled, 'These men brought out information and keys and the Fianna under Joe Robinson and Séamus Reader constantly raided for explosives. The years leading up to 1916 in Glasgow and the daring, the astuteness and the ease with which even Scotland Yard was "codded" is an episode that should someday be written.'

Through a network of family, friends and Republican contacts spanning Glasgow and Belfast, Joe had a well-established supply line to facilitate arms, ammunition and explosives importation to Ireland. Many of these weapons and explosives would subsequently be used during the Easter Rising. Séumas Robinson noted:

> I believe Joe himself was prepared for a life of hardship and excitement with a hangman's rope likely at the end. However, I had my own ideas but didn't mention them to Joe. I was always anxious to know how serious the movement was and I learned by trial and error a method to find out. The only way I could get Joe to talk was to throw cold water on their bona-fides. Then he told me in so positive, cool, matter of fact way that a fight would come off, not only in our time, but very shortly, that I believed him.

Joe and his comrades in the Fianna continued with their quest for weapons and explosives. These activities continued unabated until January 1916. After a raid on the magazine of a Lanarkshire colliery, evidence was allegedly found implicating Joe Robinson. According to British Intelligence Notes, 'Robinson was known to the police in Glasgow as a Captain in the Irish Volunteers there, and a man holding very extreme views.' The Special Branch arrested Joe and proceeded to search the house. This raid uncovered a loaded revolver as well as a telegram from 'Reader' handed in at Dublin stating 'Arrived safe and well.'

Séamus Reader was also arrested and both were charged with 'Larceny of explosives from Messrs Adie and sons between 2pm on Saturday 15 January and 8am on Sunday 16 January 1916.' Each of them was given a lengthy jail sentence. This episode was a significant turning point in the life of Séumas Robinson; after Joe's arrest, 'the sabotage in the shipyards and the raids for explosives that had been going on (several submarines never came up on their first trial) and other destruction which had previously been attributed to the Anarchists was now rightly attributed to us, and we were therefore very much on-the-run...'

A solution to his predicament came when 'our IRB centre, Tom McDonnell, told us that all able-bodied young men with engineering experience were to report at once to Dublin.' Séumas Robinson was forced, by circumstance, from an ancillary role to what was to become the frontline. With a now singular focus, Robinson was to take an active role in the coming fight for Irish Freedom. He articulated the measures he adopted to ensure readiness:

I prepared myself mentally and physically. I trained myself to be supple not muscle-bound, and I found my strength increasing markedly. I learned to jump my own height - only 5' 6" - but it was tough going. I learned to sprint with all my clothes on in short bursts of 20 to 30 yards. I learned to shoot. My father had already taught me the theory of shooting and Joe had an air-rifle from our Belfast days and I took every opportunity of practice at circus and show grounds and at rifle ranges. I was very proud the first time I hit the ball dancing on the water fountain. I became quite good judging by what I saw round about me. I discovered with secret delight that the average British Tommy was quite a poor shot. I may have been unfortunate in those I came across. I had gained a confidence that later experience showed was not quite justified. I hadn't yet learned the need to be "quick on the draw" and that one had to be either "the quick or the dead."

No amount of training could quite prepare him for the coming experiences that would unfold in Dublin. He was to receive quite the 'baptism of fire' and earn his 'spurs' during the planned nationwide insurgency that was scheduled for Easter 1916.

CHAPTER TWO

A BAPTISM OF FIRE

From preparation to action, Dublin: January – April 1916

Following the arrests of Joe Robinson and Séamus Reader, things began to heat up in Scotland for the Volunteers. According to Séumas Robinson, 'In desperation the Scots Police Authorities called in Maguire and Hannigan (the two Dublin Castle political G men appointed to watch the Irish in Scotland) for consultation. These two fellows guessed immediately who was behind the raids.' More arrests were planned, so it was imperative that any Volunteers who were able to get out went straight to Ireland.

After successfully dodging the watchful eyes of the G Men, the Scottish Volunteers arrived in Dublin without incident. Here they were christened 'The Refugees,' and their new home was located at the 'Kimmage Garrison.' This was part of Count Plunkett's estate, *Larkfield*. His family were all active in the Republican Movement. Most of the members of the 'Garrison' were Irishmen who had fled Britain in order to escape arrest or avoid conscription into the British Army, choosing instead to fight for Ireland. Strangely, some of these men were second generation Irish and had never set foot in the country before their arrival in Dublin. During the ensuing Rising many of their Cockney, Mancunian, Liverpudlian and Glaswegian accents raised many eyebrows in the streets of the capital city as they were commandeering supplies or occupying buildings in the name of an Irish Republic.

The atmosphere at Kimmage was distinctly martial in tone. The inhabitants were engaged in full-scale preparation for the expected insurrection. A sort of mini Krupp's production line was in operation. The men were employed to make cases for bombs from billycans, 'funny looking bayonets' for shotguns and a vast quantity of buckshot. Séumas Robinson remembered one mishap they had when trying to make their own firearms:

> At least once we even attempted to make a gun. There was something of a joke in this gun making business, and I spiked the gun literally in order to spike it metaphorically. George Plunkett wanted a long-range buckshot gun, which simply could be made out of a piece of malleable iron piping – even though it be called "gun metal." The charge was doubled and jammed tightly. The gun was fired. I have heard of Peter Pan losing his shadow and getting it back again, when that gun went off, I thought that I had lost my zenith… something nearly hit me.

Things were at full tilt for the coming insurgency but not everything was going to pan out as planned; therefore, the 1916 Easter Rising went 'off at half cock.' A projected arms landing in County Kerry had gone disastrously wrong, resulting in the capture of Roger Casement and the deaths of a number of Volunteers who drove off the pier at Ballykissane while they were on their way to capture a wireless station at Valentia Island. Unbeknown to both the German Admiralty and the IRB, British Naval Intelligence knew about the arms landing after they had broken the German radio codes. The ship was intercepted and the German Captain scuttled the vessel along with its cargo of 20,000 rifles, machine guns and ammunition.

The planned insurrection was to be the culmination of IRB policy since the revitalisation of the separatist organisation in the early 1900s. A secret Military Council, who was tasked to organise the rebellion, devised a strategy of infiltrating and directing other groups such as the Irish Volunteers towards their desired end of an insurrection. When Éoin Mac Néill, Chief of Staff of the Volunteers, discovered their plans, coupled with the arms capture, he cancelled all mobilisation orders for Easter Sunday. Hence, according to historian JJ Lee, 'the hastily rearranged Rising that began on Easter Monday was not, therefore the intended insurrection.' Another historian, JA Murphy, reinforces this view and points out that circumstances ensured that the 'projected nationwide rebellion dwindled to one in Dublin and one or two other isolated attempts elsewhere. When the Blood Sacrifice aspect of the Easter Rising … took the place of a planned military venture.'

There was a feeling of anticipation amongst the members of the 'Kimmage Garrison.' They were hoping to escape the doldrums; life in the garrison was only mildly exciting, and there were no luxuries such as baths. So, when the cancellation order came through on Easter Sunday disappointment reigned, a collective groan reverberated around *Larkfield*.

However, Séumas Robinson observed on Easter Monday morning George Plunkett's demeanour had changed. 'He was wearing a broad, proud, confident smile and a sword!' He soon gave the order to the garrison to parade with full equipment and rations. The rank and file were still unaware that something was afoot as they marched toward Dolphin's Barn Tram Terminus.

The 'Kimmage Garrison' had now set out for Dublin on Easter Monday morning. With a long march ahead of them, it was decided to commandeer a tram. Robert Kee in his history of Ireland recorded the famous incident of when 'George Plunkett came up the stairs of the tram in place of the conductor to count the numbers accurately, and then paid all their fares in full. The incident is symptomatic of the strange mixture of amateurism and deadly intent that characterised so much of that spasmodic day of the Rising.'

They alighted at College Green and marched onward to the bustle and excitement of Liberty Hall. Séumas Robinson was informed by Margaret Skinnider, a Cumann na mBan activist originally from Glasgow, that "It's on" and as he marched along the quays, he felt like he was walking on air:

> ...when the Rebellion did not come off on Sunday there was growls and mumblings amongst ourselves; but it came off on Monday and all was well. Some of us burned our papers, we would soldier on for the rest of our lives or until Ireland was free. We thought the Germans would help and that the country would rise with us.

Through the streets of Dublin marched companies of Irish Volunteers, members of the Citizen Army, Cumann na mBan and Fianna Éireann. 'The marching contingents were a familiar sight and occasioned no unusual interest,' but it was towards noon when Dubliners knew that something more than a route march was afoot when a shot rang out at the gate of Dublin Castle, the seat of British administration in Ireland. During an attempt to capture the building shots were exchanged with British Army officers. An unarmed Dublin Metropolitan Police constable was killed, soon afterwards Seán Connolly was also shot dead. The first casualties of the Rising had occurred.

Buildings were occupied all over the city. Foraging parties were sent out to commandeer food, bedding and medical supplies, 'many of them offering in return receipts promising compensation by the Irish Republic but most were received with ill grace by local shop and hotel managers.'

From outside Dublin's General Post Office, occupied as the Headquarters of the Provisional Government, the Proclamation of the Irish Republic was read aloud to a somewhat bemused and bewildered audience:

POBLACHT NA H EIREANN THE PROVISIONAL GOVERNMENT OF THE IRISH REPUBLIC TO THE PEOPLE OF IRELAND. IRISHMEN AND IRISHWOMEN In the name of God and the dead generations from which she receives her old tradition of nationhood, Ireland, through us, summons her children to her flag and strikes for her freedom...

Events in Dublin 'dumbfounded general opinion...many accounts exist that record astonishment, derision and occasional inspiration.' Indeed, the British Authorities were taken completely unaware. It was thought after the arms capture in Kerry and Mac Néill's countermanding order that everything was cancelled. Contained within Dublin Castle Records are reports from two highly placed agents within Irish Volunteers circles, codenamed 'Chalk' and 'Granite,' to the G Division or political detectives of the Dublin Metropolitan Police. Both had given an indication of the looming insurrection, but these agents had not successfully infiltrated that secret stratum of the inner circle of IRB leaders within the Irish Volunteers and so seemed unaware of the rearranged plan for Easter Monday. This in part explains the initial surprise achieved by the insurgents.

The Rising had begun in earnest. James Connolly proudly declared that the insurgents should no longer look upon themselves as Irish Volunteers or Citizen Army but as the Irish Republican Army.

Séumas Robinson was promoted to Second Lieutenant and placed in command of a small section of Volunteers. On the way to O'Connell Street Bridge Peadar Bracken, another Kimmage man who had been on-the-run since a shootout with the RIC at

Tullamore earlier in the year, showed Robinson an order signed by James Connolly. This order stipulated that Kelly's Gun Store, also known as the Fort, at the corner of Bachelors Walk and O'Connell Street and Hopkins & Hopkins Jewellery Shop at the opposite corner on Eden Quay were to be seized as outposts to protect the approach to the GPO from O'Connell Bridge.

Robinson halted his section on the bridge and explained their task:

> I wondered how long it would be in bursting into a burglar proof jewellers' shop – steel shutters all around…in the meantime I held up a mountain of a DMP man. With my little shotgun I must have looked like a Lilliputian threatening Gulliver with a peashooter. I had to break into something bordering on blasphemy before I could get that good natured and only mildly scarred Bobby to stand aside until we could get inside the building.

The DMP officer during the course of his duty became quite curious as to the motives of a number of armed men trying to break into a jewellery shop. When the penny dropped and he realised that an armed rebellion was underway, discretion became the better part of valour: "'Oh! I see. Well you boys needn't worry about me I won't interfere. In my opinion this is a matter for the military.'"

These small, but crucially important, outposts were eventually established. The occupants set about tunnelling into adjacent premises. Séumas Robinson, while supervising the fortification of the building, noticed a party of British Troops on horseback coming down Eden Quay towards him. He remembered when:

> …glancing along Eden Quay, I saw a large body of cavalry coming in my direction. Heavens! Now I stood for an

instant, marvelling that the British could not have got word and have acted so quickly. I could see none of my men. A dictionary may define panic, but at that moment I knew what it was.

Finally, here was the first test for the young insurgent. He immediately and instinctively went to confront this mounted menace. 'I realised at once that I was not too cowardly (though I had often previously wondered how I would react to danger) because I was willing (though I had no liking for it) to put my body and it's miserable little shotgun with composition bayonet between the Calvary and the GPO.'

Mixed emotions were a significant feature of Easter Week 1916. Robinson recalled, 'I have always dreaded being, or even appearing to be ridiculous...it surely made me feel ridiculous to the passer-by when they beheld a little fellow looking grim – at least I felt that way – lying flat on the road in the slight protection of the foot kerb, with his little gun aimed at the halted column of Calvary.'

From his vantage point on the roadway, Séumas Robinson observed an exchange with the British Soldiers:

Some elderly gentleman in a motor car, who had passed the G.P.O. and had seen what was happening, dashed up to the cavalry as they came on to O'Connell Street, and was soon holding up the cavalry leader and gesticulating towards the G.P.O., evidently telling the officer all about it. The leader looked up O'Connell Street once or twice, then shook his head and pointed over his shoulder. In moments of real danger how quick and clear instinct becomes. I saw as clearly as if I had heard him speak the words, that soldier say he was in charge of a party escorting something, and was simply under orders to do just that job.

He shook the reins and moved off, crossing O'Connell Street from Eden Quay to Bachelors Walk and on to the Four Courts, where they were met with fire. The Volunteers there were evidently in possession by the time the cavalry reached the Four Courts.

One Dubliner commented "'Those fellows are not going to be frightened by a troop of lancers. They mean business.'"

Séumas Robinson encountered more problems. Within the fortified Hopkins' premises, there were now only three Volunteers, including Robinson himself. The rest had panicked at the sight of the soldiers and made a dash for the GPO. Robinson and his two comrades, Séamus Lundy from Liverpool and Cormac Turner a fellow Glasgow Battalion man, were to go through the mill over the next few days. They sent word over to the GPO that only three Volunteers were holding the block of buildings from O'Connell Bridge to the premises of the Dublin Bread Company. No reinforcements were forthcoming and things were looking pretty ominous for the small contingent of Volunteers.

The first day of the Rising was relatively quiet. The rebels on Easter Monday 'took not only the Castle authorities, but most of Dublin by surprise.' A major criticism was this unpreparedness, with one British official noting that 'Everyone believed that the point was off the Irish pikes, and the gunmen had forgotten how to shoot.' However, the British soon got their act together, and troops began pouring into Dublin in order to crush the rebellion.

They threw a cordon around Dublin and slowly began to tighten it. The fight would soon intensify for Séumas Robinson and his comrades. It was to be an extremely chaotic week of dodging bombs, bullets and incendiary shells. In Robinson's words a literal 'baptism of fire':

The week was a hectic one, especially whenever we had to cross to the G.P.O. under machine gun fire. It became so dangerous that I had to do most of my own messages. A bit foolish, though, for an O/C. to do but, after all, perhaps the whole fight was rather foolish from a military point of view. It became much too hot when the buildings (I think ours was the first to be set on fire in the G.P.O. area) began to crackle.

The insurgents expected a textbook frontal military assault entailing close quarter fighting; hence, they were armed with shotguns. After entering the building, Robinson recalled that 'we made what barricades we could on the ground floor, and waited all day for the charge we expected to take place at any moment.' But the attack did not come in the manner they thought.

James Connolly, Military Commander of the insurgent forces in Dublin, felt that the ruling British capitalist class would not unleash the destructive force of artillery to level Dublin, the second city of their Empire. He would soon be proven wrong and by Tuesday the start of the serious fighting began.

In the first instance the British military began to use snipers and concentrated heavy machine gun fire from Trinity College towards O'Connell Street. This rendered the men at Hopkins' corner impotent. All they could do was to continue tunnelling through the walls down towards Abbey Street. Séumas Robinson went to the GPO and sought out George Plunkett to outline their perilous position. Plunkett stated to Robinson that there were no spare personnel but gave an undertaking that he would see what he could do. Robinson returned to his post. British bullets were flying; the intensity was increasing.

Plunkett managed to get a crack shot sniper, Andy Conroy of the Citizen Army, sent over to join Robinson to try and alleviate the situation. 'His accuracy from the roof of Hopkins and Hopkins soon slowed but did not stop the fire from Trinity.'

The building shook, and a haze of dust and debris filled the air. The British had begun to use artillery. The pace of the fighting steadily increased, and a continual fire was directed against Hopkins' corner. The insurgents, held in static positions and numerically smaller, were fighting on the defensive. Maryann Gialanella Valiulis, in her study of Richard Mulcahy, astutely observed that this was 'the type of military situation which makes it almost impossible for those with smaller numbers and limited amounts of arms and ammunition to win.'

Many of Dublin's poor made the precarious expedition into the streets to loot and witness the strange happenings in their city. One of these unfortunate people, a woman, was struck by a hail of machine gun bullets intended for the Volunteers in Hopkins' shop. By the time anyone reached her, the lifeblood had drained from her; she lay prostrate on the footpath.

The insurgents stationed at the two outposts spied the ominous shape of a British Naval vessel chugging up the river Liffey. Soon *The Helga* halted at Butt Bridge and began to lob artillery shells at the building that had long been a symbol of defiance and resistance to British imperialism. *Liberty Hall,* the headquarters of the Irish Transport and General Workers Union (ITGWU), which had proudly and defiantly displayed the banner WE SERVE NEITHER KING NOR KAISER BUT IRELAND, lay in ruins, a smouldering shell of its former glory. There were no insurgent forces occupying the building, but the British considered it a worthy target anyway.

This was not a good omen. The British cordon was tightening; word was sent over to the GPO about what was happening, but the sound of added artillery fire was unmistakable. Dublin received a pounding. Rumours were flying like the bullets that were pinging off the walls. The whole country was supposed to be in open rebellion, the British had suffered heavy casualties and the Germans had landed in support.

One anonymous account captures the intensity of the fighting, 'the whole city has awakened up. The booming of field guns can be heard from the vicinity of O'Connell Street, rifle cracks can be heard from all parts of the city.' Combat intensified further, and the same witness saw 'soldiers taking all available cover, even the limited protection a lamppost afforded them.'

The small band of brothers who held Hopkins' corner knew it was only going to be a matter of time until their outpost resembled *Liberty Hall*. Dublin began to resemble a town in Belgium or France that had been ravaged during the Great War. For the moment, the only answer to the artillery fire was the pathetic shotgun blasts from the Volunteers stationed at Kelly's Fort and Hopkins' corner.

Séumas Robinson, Cormac Turner and Séamus Lundy were coming under increasing pressure from a machine gun positioned in the turret of Tara Street Fire Station and by a sniper placed at McBirney's department store across the Liffey. The fire was so intense at one stage that the three insurgents had to eat lying flat on their stomachs. They located the sniper at the top central window. Word was sent over to Andy Conroy who had shifted position to Kelly's Fort. He promptly put the sniper out of action. As soon as this threat was eradicated, the Volunteers based at Hopkins' corner outpost recommenced their tunnelling activities, breaching the buildings going up O'Connell Street. When they reached the premises of the Dublin Bread Company, they found that a number of Volunteers were using the high domed tower as a sniping position.

Word arrived on Thursday that Commandant General James Connolly had ordered the evacuation of the block, but Séumas Robinson was reluctant to leave their post until he had received confirmation. Nevertheless, the small garrison set out for the GPO and made their evacuation from the Hibernian Bank in Abbey Street through to Marlborough and North Earl Streets and rushed towards the GPO in quadruple quick time, sheltering at the far side of Nelson's Pillar. Heavy machine gun and rifle fire was coming down O'Connell Street from the direction of Westmoreland Street, Trinity College and Mc Birney's.

Miraculously, they reached the GPO without casualties. Inside James Connolly cleared up the confusion and told them to reoccupy the block. They returned the way that they came, but this time the British had moved closer having seen them evacuating their positions. A Volunteer called Frank Scullin was hit. Séumas Robinson grabbed him; he believed that the British sniper respected what he was trying to do by helping a fallen comrade and trained his sights elsewhere. They managed to reoccupy the buildings, but heavy fire was concentrated upon them as they did so.

All the while, the British artillery rained a torrential downpour of incendiary shells upon their position. It was a blazing inferno. Séumas Robinson and his comrades had to abandon the outpost; their position was no longer tenable. 'Hopkins and Hopkins burnt - we got across to the G.P.O. on Thursday night under terrific fire and from then on I was between the G.P.O., the Metropole Hotel, Moore Lane and Moore Street.' They had to duck and dive across O'Connell Street, again sheltering at statues, kerbs, doorways and barricades; this time, Andy Conroy was hit but still managed to make it across. On reaching the GPO they found it secured, and the Volunteers on duty would not allow them in:

In fairness to the Volunteers in the G.P.O. I think it well to point out that the vast majority of the G.P.O. garrison had not been outside the precincts during the week, and by Thursday evening they had been worked up to a crisis of expectation of an assault by the British, and, the ordinary Volunteers, knowing that the buildings opposite the G.P.O. had been vacated from Wednesday, didn't know there were any Volunteers still trying to hold O'Connell Street Bridge from Hopkins & Hopkins. They must have wondered where I had come from if I was not a spy. I was held up for no more than a minute or two but it seemed like an hour. I was so annoyed that I completely forgot to be afraid.

They shouted and pleaded to be let in. They then heard some back-stage whispering until a commanding voice ordered that they be admitted. The voice belonged to James Connolly who immediately assigned them to posts within the garrison. Now within the confines of the GPO, Robinson felt an overwhelming tiredness descend. He was in dire need of some rest:

When I found myself for the first time among a crowd without any personal responsibility a sleep reaction set in: I felt overpowered from want of it. I had almost to implore a Volunteer Officer who seemed to be in charge of the beds on the ground floor. He pointed to a bed under a counter. I crept into it. I was left undisturbed from 7 p.m. until midnight when he wakened me to do sentry duty until 5 a.m., that had only been five hours sleep followed by five hours lone sentry duty. I could see no one about during those long five hours; I had to keep knocking my knuckles against a granite stone window-sill to keep awake . . . my head was swimming! But on getting a cup of tea I was thoroughly alert again.

An exhausted Séumas Robinson found inspiration in the figure of James Connolly, who was rallying the troops throughout the

GPO. Robinson noticed that Connolly had difficulty walking, and there was a trail of blood in his wake. The injured Commandant General was still making the effort, despite being wounded, to encourage and support the men and women under his command; soon, he was further injured and left in crippling pain. The courage displayed by Connolly filled Séumas Robinson with the motivation and determination to keep alert and fighting. It also left him with a lasting admiration and respect for Connolly and his ideas for the Re-conquest of Ireland. Robinson, in an account of Easter Week compiled for Ina Connolly-Heron in 1957, affectionately concluded with the description of her father as a 'man's man in every fibre of his body and mind.'

Séumas Robinson was sent to Mansfield Corner, making his way through the Metropole Hotel. A number of Volunteers were already at this outpost including two friends of Robinson, brothers Martin and Joe Gleeson. Séumas Robinson noted that:

> There was terrific firing along Abbey Street: machine-gun, rifle and 'pom-pom' fire answered during every slight lull by a loud defiant 'pong!' of a Howth gun. I was wondering why there were so few Volunteers at this most important post seeing there was a goodly number of men in the G.P.O. I spoke to some of the men on the spot; the British could have rushed this ground-floor position with half a Company.

Robinson was articulating these thoughts to his comrades. Everyone was on high alert, and he later recalled that 'Perhaps I merely helped to put the "wind up" some of the young fellows because during a longish lull of about fifteen seconds there was suddenly a loud clattering of nailed boots running across Abbey Street accompanied by another tremendous outbreak of firing and followed by a loud knocking on the door.'

The two young Volunteers stationed at the door began to back away with their rifles pointed in expectation. A voice from outside called on them to open the door. 'I nodded to the two young fellows and pointed to the door. They were in a slight crouching position, eyes glued on the door, rifles lowered as if waiting to receive charge. They uttered not a word. I shouted "Who are you!" "A Volunteer. Open the door."' Continuing with his account, Séumas Robinson captures the intense sense of trepidation and eventual relief upon finding out that it was not a contingent of British soldiers:

> I cocked my gun, finger on the trigger, pressed the gun tightly against my side to absorb the 'kick' and then I cautiously opened the door with my left hand. In strode James Connolly. It would be difficult to describe my surprise; and it would be impossible for me to describe the shock I got when he immediately began to scold me for "not being at your post which is at the sandbags." I was so nonplussed in front of the great man that all I could do was to murmur "It was not my post." Connolly heaved himself over the barricade and ambled slowly with measured tread to the Gleesons, chatted with them a moment or two, then continued on his way to the G.P.O. During all this time Connolly showed no signs of excitement or distress much less of pain. The only sign of emotion was his slight trace of anger or annoyance at my supposed delay in opening the door. At that time, I thought he was giving us all a lesson in coolness after passing through the inferno that was Abbey Street. And what a lesson that was. I didn't realise until that Friday night when I realised that he had made his way through all the buildings, over all sorts of obstacles and through all the narrow zig-zag holes in the walls from Abbey Street to Princes Street and so to the G.P.O. as if he were on a casual inspection, with his ankle shattered by a bullet or shrapnel. He hid his predicament from everyone.

Connolly appeared so unruffled that no one seemed to be aware that he was hurt much less severely crippled until Dr. Ryan had cut the boot off him… "His ankle was shattered something awful."

Robinson again found himself in the GPO as the artillery shells began to hit the building for the first time. Volunteers began to use hoses to try and quell the blaze, but this proved to be futile. Rifle and machine gun bullets now came through the windows and were ricocheting off the walls. Volunteers looked for opportunities to return fire, again expecting the British to rush the building. Everyone was in a high state of alert and a strange vibrancy transcended over the building, but the British didn't charge. Munitions were removed and explosives were taken to a lower room to be detonated after the building was evacuated.

The British cordon had finally tightened. A strangle hold pinned the insurgents in their positions; they needed to break loose. Attempted breaches were made, but this strategy was highly precarious and the majority of rebel fatalities occurred during these efforts. Connolly was wounded again and *The O'Rahilly*, who was opposed to the Rising but expressed the opinion 'I have helped to wind the clock now I will hear it strike,' was killed while leading a charge away from the GPO.

The rebels needed to move in short, sharp bursts. Séumas Robinson was charged with leading a contingent from HQ and he vacated the GPO by a side door in Henry Street. 'By this time, we advanced a great deal nearer the British barricade in Moore Street and the charge would not have been quite so Balaclava-like as the previous ones.'

Shelter was sought in Moore Street and groups of Volunteers crowded into a house. Séumas Robinson recalled seeing Connolly on a stretcher. He seemed cheerful and waved over to him saying, "Hello Townie." Connolly had been informed by one of the Gleeson brothers who Robinson was, and "Townie" was a reference to their mutual connection to Belfast. 'I suppose (also I Hope!) the Gleesons also cleared me of any blame for the delay in letting him in at Abbey Street!!'

Volunteers began to bore through the walls using a large crowbar. Each Volunteer took a turn at the bar for a few minutes, then stopped for a rest while a fresh man took over. The scene all around them was a blazing holocaust of fire and rubble; the Volunteers had to try one final push. A small group led by Séumas Robinson raced along the back alleys toward Amiens Street. Everywhere they were confronted by figures in khaki and eventually with nowhere left to run, they found themselves in a narrow alleyway, which possessed a dead end. TH Coffey, in his book *Agony at Easter*, captures the last gasping moments of involvement that Séumas Robinson and his comrades had in the Rising; 'Stopping, out of breath, they waited helplessly, listened to the approach of hobnailed boots, caught glimpses in the dark. Any moment the first gun would fire and dozens of bullets would riddle them as they stood against the dead-end wall.'

Luckily for the Volunteers, the soldiers who confronted them in the darkness had only arrived as reinforcements. They had not experienced the trauma of the week, so Robinson and his comrades were spared from summary execution. One of the British soldiers said "'A scruffy lot, aren't they?" Another laughed nervously. Moving forward they grabbed the guns from the cornered insurgents, and the Hopkins and Hopkins men ended their part in the rebellion with more than they had reason to hope for, their lives.'

The overall situation was hopeless, and Pearse issued a surrender order. After almost a week, the rebellion was crushed; it seemed a failure. All the leaders were captured, mass arrests were made and people from all over Ireland were interned. Executions of the leaders followed, and the course of Irish history would be changed. The tide began to turn in favour of the Republicans. For Séumas Robinson, this was just a warm-up; his fight had only just begun. He had earned what he called his 'spurs in the holocaust of fires that was Easter Week.' Facing an unwelcome sojourn in prison he was, nevertheless, determined to soldier on until Ireland was free and he would go to wherever the fight took him.

CHAPTER THREE

THEY SHALL NOT HAVE FOUGHT AND DIED IN VAIN

From Imprisonment to Reorganisation:
April 1916 – December 1918

After the surrender of the insurgent forces in Dublin on the Saturday, the Volunteers were marched in formation into O'Connell Street. All those still in possession of arms surrendered them here. Everyone was subsequently herded into the Rotunda Gardens where they spent the night without cover.

On Sunday, the Volunteers were moved from the Rotunda to Richmond Barracks and housed in a large gymnasium. People were processed individually through a large interrogation room. Each was screened by Political Detectives, or G Men as they were known, to ascertain if they were rank and file or held leadership positions. Some men were subsequently separated and housed in large rooms throughout the barracks while others were taken away for immediate deportation. Robinson remembered, 'After the surrender I was held back in Richmond Barracks for about a week while all my fighting companions were shipped to England. I do not know why I was held; what I do know is that a big "G" man, on hearing my name, pounced on me and handed over to some soldiers.' Séumas Robinson was probably given special attention due his Glasgow address and the connection to Joe, who was already well known to the political detectives. Housed in the same room were Pádraig Ó

Máille, Joseph Gleeson, Joseph Derham, Séamus Mallin, MW O'Reilly, Barney Mellows, Frank Fahy, Major John McBride (later executed) and AP Reynolds. Robinson was then deported to Stafford Gaol in England after being held in Richmond Barracks for about a week.

As his official residence was listed as Glasgow, he fell under the parameters of the Conscription Act. The British Authorities attempted to press any of the men with addresses in Scotland or England into the British Army and thus into the trenches of the Great War. These men were labelled 'Evaders,' and soon Séumas Robinson developed a reputation for steadfastly refusing to cooperate with the British Authorities and their attempts to conscript him. One prisoner, TD Sinnott, recorded that 'If few in the first two weeks knew Séumas Robinson then everybody in Stafford Gaol knew the small, little man of steel with the russet stubble and shy retiring manner within days of the issue of the yellow form.' This paperwork was a questionnaire asking the men to detail their activities during Easter Week. Robinson point blankly refused to fill this in or to sign his internment order.

A Commission under the chairmanship of Sir John Sankey was established to examine the individual cases of the Irish prisoners, including those who were deemed eligible for military service in the British armed forces or to determine whether their detention should continue. Séumas Robinson recorded:

> None of the Glasgow Battalion boys ever tried to hide his identity in the camps. We had all previously agreed among ourselves that when we would appear before the Sankey Commission, we would tell the chairman that we wanted neither mercy nor anything else from him or his government, unless and except a rifle in our hands and we'd find our own targets, no matter where we were, be it at the front or rear. The bluff worked. True, the War Office had

had two years experience of the Glasgow "desperados" and I am informed that the War Office sent word not to interfere with us. Not one of us, then or ever after, was threatened with conscription, and that fact itself lends colour to all I have said about the Glasgow Battalion. The London and Liverpool men were harried.

Deemed a disruptive influence, Robinson was moved to Frongoch internment camp in Wales. He even disrupted the transportation process. One fellow prisoner, James Kavanagh, recalled:

> I was told a very funny story about one of the prisoners – Séumas Robinson. I was told he was to have gone in the first batch but he was almost naked as his clothes were completely worn away. The rough usage had been too much for them. The British Army Commandant decided to provide him with a top coat to cover his nakedness while marching through the town and asked him to sign a receipt for it. Séumas refused. He said he'd sign nothing. The Commandant argued with him for a considerable time, but he still refused. Eventually the contingent had to go without him and he went back to his cell. I believe this went on every day until only the last contingent was left. Eventually Séumas got the coat without signing for it. The commandant gave it to him in the presence of some members of the prison staff who signed as witnesses.

Eventually, Robinson arrived in Frongoch. He was held here for around a month and was moved again to Reading Gaol for causing more disruption in the camp. The prisoners paraded outside the huts each morning for inspection. The inside of the huts were cleaned and tidied. The British Army Commandant, followed by his staff, came around and inspected everything, praising and condemning as he thought fit. One morning the men were all lined up for inspection. James Kavanagh remembered 'Séumas Robinson was housed in the hut immediately facing mine. At that time, he had a big mop of black hair and big black whiskers sticking out straight all around his face.' Apparently, Robinson looked very comical in this state of unkemptness and began, with the help of another prisoner, to act like a puppet on a string. Kavanagh sketched the comedic routine:

> The companion caught hold of his hair and Séumas started going up and down by bending his knees and keeping his body straight from the hips up. The timing was so good that you'd think he was hanging out of a piece of elastic and being jerked up and down by his pal. Naturally when we saw this, we all began to laugh. The Commandant looked round but your men were immediately standing to attention. As soon as the Commandant turned back, they were at it again, and again when he looked round, they were at attention. This went on for so long that we were almost sick with the laughing.

The prisons are often credited as the places where the blueprint for the ensuing War for Independence was drafted. Frongoch in particular is as cited as the 'University of Revolution,' the place where people like Michael Collins laid the foundations for guerrilla warfare. Séumas Robinson alludes to political talks, military lectures, networking between prisoners, etc. but was at pains to state that:

> I would say deliberately that nowhere - in camps or gaols - did anyone ever suggest how or when "a beginning must be made." It would have been foolish. No prisoner or internee knew what the conditions were like outside nor how they would develop. I have no first-hand knowledge of what took place in the convict prisons nor in Frongoch after my two or three weeks there when I was picked out

with S. T. O'Kelly, Walter Cole, N.W. O'Reilly, Tom Craven and Darrell Figgis and sent to Reading Gaol, because I was blamed for starting a strike against road-making in the Camp "unless we get Trade Union wages!" We didn't get Trade Union wages: they didn't get the roads and I was 'paid off' by being sent to Reading Gaol.

In Reading Gaol, Séumas Robinson was reunited with his brother Joe and came into contact with men like Arthur Griffith, Sean T. O'Kelly, Herbert Moore-Pimm, Darrell Figgis, George Nicholls, Seán Milroy, Ernest Blythe, Cathal O'Shannon and others, most of whom were all leaders in Sinn Féin. He remembered that it was 'only natural that the revival of Sinn Féin was Operation No. 1 with them. Most of these men had their own good sound reasons for thinking that a united passive resistance policy was all-sufficient to win Irish independence.' The younger, more militant men had a tremendous regard for the intelligence, clear-sightedness, integrity and zeal of these eminent men.

Robinson felt that common sense told him and other Volunteers:

> ...that without a strong, vigorous, vociferous political party the Army would be swamped by pro-British partisan propaganda of press and pulpit. Also, we could see the usefulness, the importance, the necessity of the moral-legal support of an elected Government, the 'Constituent Assembly' of Arthur Griffith's talks to us. We were sensible to the necessity of having the will of the people behind the coming struggle. The Volunteer Officers in Reading (men like Terence McSweeney, Tomás McCurtain, J.J. O'Connell, Éamonn Ó Duibhir, Joe Robinson, Séamus Reader, Mick Brennan, Pádraig Ó Maille) were enthusiastically in favour of the political movement as the nation's second arm for what it was worth, and it was equally with the army of vital importance to the success of a revolution.

While Robinson stated that no specific blueprint was created in the prisons for the subsequent struggle, the how and when to pick up where they had left off was foremost in their minds:

> This question is often asked: How, when and on whose authority did the hostilities begin after 1916. The "how" and the "when" would be coincidental. To take the last first: "On whose responsibility or initiative did fighting begin?" I would say that it was the leaders of the 1916 Rising by their heroic deaths after an historic fight that left us survivors (and all who were imbued with the Fenian ideal) no honourable alternative but the slogan: "They shall not have fought and died in vain."

Many of the Irish prisoners were released at Christmas 1916. Séumas Robinson was amongst them. He had decided not to return to Glasgow. 'By the way I should like to add, even emphasise, I had made up my mind I'd never leave Ireland again should I have to beg my bread, and I would willingly sweep the streets.' He wanted to play his part in reorganising and rebuilding the Volunteers and help in renewing hostilities to obtain Irish Freedom.

After the releases from internment, Robinson felt that the Volunteers knew the political movement had such immense support from the people as a whole that it was unnecessary for them to expend their time on it. They were instead able to concentrate all their energies on military preparations.

Sinn Féin and political gatherings often became the cloak for Volunteer meetings. The first Volunteer Convention after 1916 was held under the cover of a Sinn Féin meeting held in October, 1917. Robinson remembered that at the Convention there was no mention of the renewal of hostilities. He estimated that the number attending would have been between 300 and 400, representing only the units then existing. No wonder, Robinson believed, that there would be no thought of opening hostilities at this stage.

It was not until a later date that the first theoretical plan of campaign was mooted. It was hypothetical, in the sense that their action was conditional on possible British moves, either wholesale arrests or the introduction of conscription. Robinson wrote, 'If fighting broke out anywhere it was up to the Volunteers everywhere to strike at everything and anything, cut communications and disrupt British movements. There was no suggestion of the Volunteers taking the initiative.'

Séumas Robinson also believed that 'The I.R.B. had lost prestige after Easter Week 1916, their authority moribund where not already dead. Many had, apparently, shirked the Rising. There had been some movement started in Frongoch which aimed at reviving and getting a change in control of the I.R.B.' He went on to recall the circumstances where he finally decided to sever all ties with the 'Organisation':

Shortly after the releases from internment young chaps mixed among us broadcasting the news that every member of the 'Organisation' was requested to attend a meeting in Parnell Square - No. 44, I think. At that meeting I saw young fellows with notebooks rushing round and about the ground floor (there were about 150 present) button-holing individuals with anxious whispers – "We must make sure that no one will be elected an officer of the Volunteers who is not a member of the 'Organisation'" – as if that were something new or something that we would be allowed to forget, and without adverting to the fact that that sort of thing would undermine the authority and efficiency of the whole Volunteer Movement. Without waiting for the meeting to start officially I walked out in disgust thinking of Tammany Hall. I never again bothered about the I.R.B. After the election of the Volunteer Executive in October 1917, whatever authority the I.R.B. retained became redundant and illegal for the Volunteers. After the first meeting of the First Dáil it had only a nuisance 'value' to the whole Movement.

Robinson's criticism of the IRB went further and he believed that after the Oath of Allegiance to the Dáil the 'Organisation' became 'a sinister cabal' manipulating the legitimate Government of the Republic. He believed in a popular, democratic movement with the moral authority and support of the people behind it.

While in Reading Gaol, Séumas Robinson would meet Éamon Ó Duibhir from Ballagh in County Tipperary. On learning that Robinson was determined not to return to Glasgow, he invited him to Tipperary to assist in the reorganisation of the Volunteer Movement there, an invitation Séamus Robinson readily accepted. He departed for Tipperary after a short stay with Arthur Griffith in Dublin. Armed with tremendous enthusiasm and influenced by his experiences during Easter Week, he had definite notions on how to conduct the fight in the next round of hostilities. Robinson recalled in his Witness Statement:

> I had been invited to go to Tipperary by Eamon Ó Duibhir while we were in Reading Gaol, to help reorganise the Volunteers if and when we were released. I had accepted gladly because I had taken a solemn resolution on Easter Monday morning, when we were sure the Rising was definitely on, that I'd soldier on for the rest of my life or until we had our freedom. During that week I realised the foolishness of being a target for overwhelming British forces. I saw what casualties could be inflicted by snipers and that the British were not averse to using any weapon

against us: they burned us out. It became abundantly clear to me that we could hope to survive and win only if we were a Ghostly Army of Sharpshooters operating all over the country combining to deal with small bodies of the enemy and making Ireland too costly to hold; always choosing our own ground, and our own targets, and always avoiding any move initiated by the British unless we had inside information and could surprise them, which would be tantamount to choosing our own ground. Succinctly: make the King's writ <u>Run</u> in Ireland.

Ó Duibhir set about making the necessary preparations for the endeavours that lay ahead. He purchased a farm house at Kilshenane, which would act as a base for their activities. The farm served as cover for all the comings and goings. When he had everything ready; Ó Duibhir sent for Séumas Robinson. There is some confusion about the exact date. Ó Duibhir believed it was January 1917, while Mick Davern put it down as late February or early March. Robinson, in his pension application firmly states that it was in March.

Mick Davern was sent to Goold's Cross Railway Station to pick up Séumas Robinson. He had borrowed a horse and cart from a sympathiser. Davern soon met Robinson and with a degree of humour he recalled their trip to Kilshenane:

From the description I had got I had no trouble in picking him [Robinson] up. Our mode of conveyance was a pony and cart which was loaned by Sam Hudson, a travelling showman, whose circus was encamped nearby. The pony had been trained to perform all sorts of circus stunts, and at regular intervals on the journey home from Goold's Cross, she would rear up on her hind legs, pirouette right round, cart and all, without causing the slightest damage, and then she would quietly continue on the journey.

Hailing from a city background, Robinson was perplexed at the antics of the horse. After the second or third 'stunt' by the pony, Séumas inquired, with a puzzled look in his eyes, if all the horses in Tipperary behave like this one? Davern reassured him that this horse was unique, and Robinson remarked '"Thank goodness!" I expect I'll have a lot to do with animals in the future, and, in order to allay the possible suspicions of the R.I.C. as to my real reason for coming to Tipperary, I'll have to learn enough to make it appear that I'm really holding down my position as a farmer's help...'

Éamon Ó Duibhir recalled that:

> Robinson arrived...in the midst of a snow storm, and he had with him a small black travelling bag that we got to know very well and to associate with him. As a farm worker, he made up for his lack of knowledge by his honesty, hustle and zeal. He certainly worked as hard as he could and left nothing undone that he could do, and in addition to all that he was a very gentlemanly man.

Davern remarked that the next morning Séumas Robinson embarked on his new mode of life, and his cover as an agricultural worker became something of an inside joke:

> Not knowing how much Séumas knew about farming, or how little he knew, he was asked would he tackle up the ass for the journey to the Creamery. He put the britchen, which should have gone on the donkey's back, right over its head, put the straddle on its back, put the donkey under the cart and connected the britchen chains to the shafts. He then informed Éamon that he couldn't find any place to put "these things." "These things" were the collar and HAMES. Many a time and oft since then we poked fun at Séumas about "these things" long after we had elected him our first

and only elected officer in command of the famous 3rd (South) Tipperary Brigade of the I.R.A. It did not take him long to commence the work for which he had come to Tipperary. We were soon discussing the formation of a section of the Volunteers. At that time, we had to be most careful who we'd ask to join us. We paraded the first time with about 15 men. Séumas drilled us on Clareen Road near Ballydine. After some weeks he appointed me Section Commander. He instilled into our minds very forcefully that he intended "this section to be the Premier Section in the Premier County." I think after events proved his hope to be justified, as it grew to be one of the largest Companies in the Brigade area.

Thomas Davis, Irish Patriot and Young Irelander, writing in *The Nation* during the 1840s, described Tipperary as the 'Premier County' due to the nationalistic sympathies of the people. He wrote 'Where Tipperary leads, Ireland follows.' The population in the county still held this patriotic outlook and were supportive to the cause of Irish Freedom. Indeed, the local Volunteers were anxious to be to the forefront of any renewed fighting as they had missed out in taking part in the Easter Rising. Robinson remembered, with a hint of wit, that:

The Volunteers there were just wild because the Rebellion had come and gone and nothing had happened in proud Tipperary. What goaded the Volunteers more than anything else was the parody on "The Soldier's Song" which the British soldier elements used to sing on the least provocation – "Soldiers are we, who nearly fought for Ireland." To their credit be it said, the Volunteers saw the humour of it, felt it in fact, and were anxious to redeem the implied stigma.

With what Ó Duibhir referred to as 'honesty, hustle and zeal,' Séumas Robinson threw himself wholesale into the reorganisation of the Republican Movement in South Tipperary. While there were many able, determined and committed people in the ranks, Robinson brought something different. Some of the local Volunteers recognised his tremendous energy and credit him with vastly enhancing the reorganisation of the area, bringing forth a new dynamic and a fresh perspective to their work.

Robinson, too, recalled that there was something special happening in Tipperary at that time. He wrote:

> What a splendid soil, what a glorious atmosphere to find oneself in! I gave a talk on my own experiences in Easter Week in the hall in Ballagh, and I declare that, when it was finished, the crowd would have rushed at and stormed anything, anywhere with hurling sticks. No wonder we made great progress.

In Tipperary the Volunteers now had, via their emerging leadership, sense, purpose and direction. The British authorities began to notice what was going on. At this critical time, Éamon Ó Duibhir was arrested under the Defence of the Realm Act and imprisoned. These regulations were designed to disrupt activities in Ireland by effectively interning key personnel. Ó Duibhir was concerned about the effect his arrest would have on reorganising in the locality but he recorded that, 'As far as the organisations were concerned, I need not have worried, for Robinson, although new to the place and unknown, had stepped into the gap and with the help of Tadhg O'Dwyer, Michael Sheehan, Bill O'Dwyer and others carried on very well.'

With the slaughter in the trenches of the Western Front and a decline in numbers forwarding themselves for service, conscription became a distinct possibility in Ireland. This galvanised public opinion squarely against the British authorities and rallied people to the Republican Standard. The ranks of the Volunteers swelled. Robinson and his comrades were working towards formalising structures in the locality and they focused on the bigger picture of creating a Brigade with functioning Battalions and Companies, an infrastructure for their own future war effort.

Arming and equipping this fledgling Volunteer organisation became essential. Weapons were sourced from friends, supporters and sympathizers. Indeed, some weapons were even unearthed that had been dumped during the Fenian years. Desmond Ryan notes that these 'venerable weapons' were actually used in the area. British soldiers were induced to part with their weapons. This became so endemic that soldiers on furlough were no longer permitted to take weapons with them. Once all these avenues were exhausted the homes of those opposed to the ideals of Irish Freedom soon became the target for raids. Mick Davern recalled, 'We were fully mindful of the necessity of getting arms and when we had collected any old weapons we could get from friendly people; we had decided to raid the homes of hostile people.' Some of these homes were reputed to be storing weapons for the unionist Ulster Volunteer Force. Séumas Robinson fully encouraged these activities and participated in many of the raids. Davern recalled in detail the first such raid carried out:

> The house of Major Edwards of Rathduff was selected for our first attempt, as we had received information that there were Carson rifles stored there. We selected a Sunday night... we decided on a ruse. It was arranged that Bill Dwyer (Sonny), an All-Ireland hurler - who later became captain of our local company would fit the bill, trusting in his powerful physique to hold any possible opposition until

the main body, who were hidden close at hand, could reach the open door in time. Bill knocked at the door and, when questioned through the closed door, said he had a sample of oats which he wanted the Major to buy, as the money was urgently needed to stave off bailiffs who were to arrive at his father's farm the next day. When the maid, an Austrian girl, conveyed this message, the Major came down and opened the door. Dwyer immediately seized him and the rest of us were at the door at once. The maid came to the Major's rescue with a large nickel-plated .45 revolver which was used to destroy crippled animals. The revolver was immediately seized by Séumas Robinson. This revolver was to play an important part in the War of Independence from Soloheadbeg. We always claimed that (though Séumas was the Brigadier and had captured the revolver himself, being the first to rush into the hall when the maid panicked and dropped it) – because it was an 'A' Company operation – that the revolver was Company property. When Séumas had risen to the automatic and parabellum stage, he 'graciously' let us have our own property back. The revolver was a nickle-plated .45 and was the one used by Séumas Robinson at Soloheadbeg some months afterwards. There were no other arms in the Major's house. He told us he detested men like Carson and Larkin who stirred up trouble in the country. Enemies spread the report that the I.R.A. had manhandled the Major and wrought destruction on the premises, but Major Edwards publicly denied this and declared that we had acted throughout the raid like gentlemen.

Drilling, marching and 'seditious' speeches continued. Séumas Robinson was now firmly under notice by the RIC in the locality. His movements were observed, and notes were made about speeches he made and the activities he led. The local RIC recorded that 'Robinson is also of extreme views and is said to have taken part in the Easter Week Rising. He is a mechanic of some sort and is believed to belong to the North of Ireland or Scotland, but is staying presently with Edward Dwyer (Kate) at Kilshenane.'

After one such 'illegal gathering' at Dundrum, it was decided to arrest Robinson. The reorganisation of the area had progressed massively and, having formed various Battalions, they were on the verge of achieving their desired goal of establishing a fully-fledged South Tipperary Brigade. His arrest in May 1918 put Séumas Robinson out of commission at this vital juncture and would impact on the formal establishment of the Brigade by a few months.

Robinson was put on trial. He did not recognise the authority of the British Court. Davern recalled what transpired at the proceedings:

> At his trial in Dundrum, Séumas informed the R.M. [Resident Magistrate] that he (the R.M.) had no moral right to try him or any other Irish citizen in Ireland because "English law in Ireland is illegitimate." To show his contempt for the Court he sang all through the trial. When singing the "Soldier's Song" he would point to the R.M. when he reached "the despot" and then at the R.I.C. when he sang "slaves." He also sang "My Dark Rosaleen." When he was released, we poked fun at Séumas: "You deserved your six months in gaol for singing that sacred song in such a desecrated place."

Robinson also remembered the joke well and remarked that 'I was sentenced to six months in Belfast jail for drilling. Some of our cute boys maintained that I got, and deserved, the six months for daring to sing "My Dark Rosaleen" in the Court during the trial. We had a glorious fight in Belfast Jail, which I enjoyed nearly as well as Easter Week.'

Séumas Robinson found himself back in his native city. Transferred from Cork Gaol, he found himself in the company of many prisoners from Munster in 'The Crum.' This was part of a policy to detach men from the areas where they had been active.

The Republican Prisoners in Belfast had been protesting about conditions and demanded political status. The atmosphere was tense. Some small outbreaks of violence precipitated a mass mutiny that would erupt when a prisoner was removed for a misdemeanour offence and lodged within general population. The Officer Commanding the Republican Prisoners, Austin Stack, demanded the return of their comrade. The Governor refused. The scene was set for a mass confrontation; Éamon Ó Duibhir takes up the story:

> Sometime later, who arrived in Belfast but Séumas Robinson, complete with his well-known travelling bag, and Ben Hickey, both direct from Kilshenane and after getting a sentence at a Special Court in Dundrum. The Governor in Belfast Prison was a harmless poor man who would be decent enough in ordinary times, but he was dealing with a tough situation and occasionally made mistakes which resulted in there being greater rows than there need have been... when the order came from Stack, we broke the cell windows and tore holes in the side walls between the cells. Our crowd had got hold of big nails and pieces of iron. The centre walls between the cells were made of one brick only, and when you got one brick loose it was easy to pull down the remainder. We wedged the doors, and then the Governor's trouble was to get us out of the cells before the wing of the prison was wrecked. In two hundred cells this rumpus was going on and the noise was terrific it was impossible for the warders to force some of the doors as they had been wedged securely. The R.I.C. and the military were

brought into the prison and hoses were employed through the broken doors to flood out the fellows inside and force them to surrender. I was amongst the earlier ones to be captured. The cell was half flooded with water and I floated or was lugged out. I was brought down to a ground floor cell, handcuffed there and the cell door then locked. The battle raged all night, with some casualties on both sides. The struggle ended on a Sunday morning and we were defeated for the time being. All were locked in various cells once more, cells that were intact on the basement floor, which had not been occupied by us up to then. Only an occasional shout of defiance and some good rebel songs were to be heard. The cells were unlocked later. Along with military with bayonets and warders with batons we were brought to the prison chapel for Mass. With a few exceptions, we were all Catholics. We were brought to Mass in irons and we passed by some of the cells that were wrecked. When passing by the cell lately occupied by Séumas Robinson, looking in I saw his famous travelling bag floating in about two feet of water.

The situation continued like this throughout the summer. Prisoners were put on reduced diets; their movement was restricted and they were placed in restraints throughout the day. Some were even held in strait-jackets. Conditions within the prison became filthy, swarms of flies invaded the wings. Soon the Spanish flu epidemic, which swept Europe in 1918 reached the prison. The atmosphere was putrid. Windows were broken again by the prisoners to facilitate the circulation of fresh air. Through their makeshift vents, the prisoners sang and shouted out into the Belfast night but only succeeded in rousing the ire of the nuns in the nearby convent.

A delegation consisting of Church and civic leaders arrived in the prison to mediate. On inspecting the wings, Dr MacRory,

Bishop of Down and Connor, seemed suitably impressed by the damage caused to the gaol by the prisoners. An accommodation was reached eventually, and life in the prison returned to normal by the end of the year. Séumas Robinson was released towards the end of October 1918. He was eager to return to Tipperary and recommence his work with the Volunteers. His experiences in Belfast Gaol also led him to a significant conclusion: it was futile to waste time rotting in prison. He vowed never to be captured again and was determined to fight his way out of any situation, or die in the attempt.

While Robinson was incarcerated, the long-sought after ambition of forming a Brigade became reality. Tadgh Dwyer, a Battalion Officer from Dundrum, recollected:

In October, 1918, the 3rd Tipperary Brigade, was formed at a meeting of Battalion Officers from all the Battalions which had then been formed in South County Tipperary. This meeting was held in an upstairs room in Moloney's chemist shop in Tipperary Town, and Dick Mulcahy, then Chief of Staff of the Irish Volunteers, presided. Then the meeting was asked for proposals for the position of Brigade Commandant. I had no hesitation in proposing Séumas Robinson. It is quite possible that many, even a majority, of those present did not then know Séumas, who was at the time serving a term of imprisonment in Belfast Jail. I pointed out that he, having fought in the Rising of 1916, had practical experience of fighting which the remainder of us lacked, and I referred to the amount of organising and training work which he had done since he came amongst us almost two years before. My proposal was seconded by the late Tommy Donovan of Drangan, who was Commandant of the 7th Battalion and who was killed by British forces at Killenaule in March, 1921. As, far as I can recall, Séumas was elected unanimously. I certainly cannot remember any other name being proposed.

It has been implied or suggested that Robinson's appointment was instigated by Seán Treacy. While there is no doubt that Treacy did have a role in the appointment, what does come into contention is the motivation behind it. Some Tipperary Volunteers, particularly Dan Breen, imply that Treacy wanted a 'stooge' or 'yes man' in place, but this line of reasoning does not take cognisance of the close bond of comradeship that developed between both men and the respect that Treacy had for Robinson, his strategic and tactical thinking as well as his Easter Week credentials.

Since his arrival in Tipperary, Séumas Robinson had expended considerable time and effort in developing the Volunteer Organisation. This was certainly recognised locally and from most accounts Robinson's appointment was welcomed. According to Éamon Ó Duibhir, it appears the only position that was disputed was that of Quartermaster. He recalled:

> Towards the end of the year Séumas Robinson was Brigade Commandant, Seán Treacy was Brigade Vice Comdt., and Dan Breen was Brigade Quartermaster. There was some opposition to Dan Breen as Quartermaster. It came from the southern end of the county, and those delegates said that I was doing the work and why not I be appointed Quartermaster. I thanked them for their attitude but said that Dan Breen was the man, and I agreed to be Assistant Brigade Quartermaster.

Due to his incarceration, Séumas Robinson obviously did not know the finer details regarding the formation of the Brigade. He was keen to know the outcome of the meeting:

> While still in jail I heard that a Convention had been held in Tipperary to form a Brigade. On my release in October I went to Dublin. At the Plaza Hotel, Headquarters at the time,

76

I met, or saw, Michael Collins, who was just going up the stairs when I entered. "Oh, they let you out" said he. "Well, I am here anyway" I answered. I was naturally anxious to know who had been chosen Brigade O/C. Not modesty, but the merest common sense prevented me thinking for one moment that there was the least chance that a stranger like me would have been chosen to take charge of the newly formed Brigade. Mick told me that Mulcahy had just returned from the Tipperary Convention, and asked me had I heard the news. I told him that I knew a convention had been held and was anxious to know who was appointed O/C. "A fellow called Séumas Robinson" said he, grinning at my stupefaction and walking on up the stairs. I confess I was surprised, and was also pleased indeed.

The overall situation would change dramatically when Robinson returned to Tipperary. The First World War was over and so too was the threat of Conscription. Numbers began to haemorrhage from the ranks of the Volunteers. A Westminster General Election was set for December. It was to be the first election since 1910. In Ireland, the political landscape was about to be turned upside down.

All attention was firmly fixed on Sinn Féin. The party would win 73 out of 105 seats, obliterating the old Irish Parliamentary Party in the process and strengthening the demand for an Irish Republic. Tactically, Republicans stood candidates who were incarcerated by the British. Included in this group was Joe Robinson, who was once again jailed for attempts to smuggle weapons into Ireland. Standing in a northern constituency that had unionist leader Sir James Craig on the ballot paper, there was no prospect of gaining that seat.

During this period of incarceration, Joe was held in Peterhead Prison. Here, he would come into contact with revolutionary socialist John MacLean; these connections would further solidify a relationship with the Scottish Socialists/Communists and Irish Republicans. The activists of the 'Red Clydeside' would demonstrate solidarity and active support for the cause of Ireland.

The 1918 Election represented a huge victory for Sinn Féin and was an endorsement of the Republican position. Ireland had been radicalised after heavy losses in the trenches of Europe, the impact of the Easter Rising and subsequent executions along with changes to the electoral franchise and lack of emigration during the war. Ireland was a tinderbox, and soon a spark from South Tipperary would ignite the country.

The Volunteers were utilised during the election campaign, working to ensure that the Republican message was spread throughout the country. Many prominent members stood as Sinn Féin candidates and were elected. Despite being on the crest of a political wave, Robinson worried about what he termed as 'Sinn Féin pacifism' holding primacy to the detriment of armed action. He pushed for meaningful military operations in his locality:

> It did not take me long to realise that the Volunteers would have to be brought by gradual stages to the sticking point – I mean the bayonet-sticking point – and that nothing would be done by a large body of Volunteers until a lead was given by a few. The Volunteers were being arrested wholesale and without death-dealing resistance, and they could feel that these arrests and the attendant hunger strikes were a direct challenge from the British. Our difficulty was to take up that challenge in a clear and clean way which would be unmistakable and would not be a mere flash in the pan. One could hardly get a group of men to storm a barracks without some sort of a declaration, or without

permission from G.H.Q. And G.H.Q. would not give permission before the whole country was ready, yet common sense dictated that when the whole country was ready, they would probably all be in jail. It was becoming increasingly difficult to keep proud young men merely drilling and getting jailed or interned for it.

Republicans would not recognise the British parliament. Their policy was to abstain from taking their seats in Westminster and to form their own national assembly, Dáil Éireann, in Dublin. This was a direct political challenge to British Rule. While Robinson was enthusiastic about having the 'moral and legal authority' of their own government, he also felt that the formation of their own parliament could impede military operations. It would give the British an excuse to suppress the Dáil forthwith, as the two would be linked.

Robinson began to think:

> ...if one could only get the ball rolling before the Dáil met then the Dáil would not be so easily connected with what would be regarded as a regrettable incident or two (which is what the beginning of the Tan War was thought to be) and guerrilla tactics might be begun surreptitiously, developed imperceptibly, and seriously extended. But how was a beginning to be made, and in time?

An opportunity soon presented itself, and Robinson was keen to grasp it with both hands:

> My mind was occupied with these thoughts when during the Christmas of 1918 Seán Treacy, my Vice O/C came to O'Dwyer's with his fiancée (Miss May Quigley) on an official visit. When tea was over Treacy informed me that some gelignite was soon to be taken to a quarry near

Tipperary Town. He was not sure of the exact date, and added that anything from two to six police would be guarding it. He wanted to know should we capture it. I said it would be something bordering on treason not to try it.

Plans were formulated that would have serious consequences and push the country from 'public defiance to guerrilla warfare.' Ireland would soon follow where Tipperary would lead.

CHAPTER FOUR

BLAZE THE TRAIL

Firing the first shots at Soloheadbeg and life 'on-the-run' –
January to May 1919

Séumas Robinson was now the first, and would be the only democratically elected Officer Commanding the Third Tipperary Brigade of the Irish Republican Army during the Tan War. The ultimate position of responsibility for the area was now thrust upon him, a duty that he would diligently perform over the next few turbulent years. There would be many trials and tribulations along the way, but all would be faced with the steadfast resolve tempered in the fires of Easter Week, subsequently forged in the prisons and now fashioned into a steely determination that, along with committed and resolute comrades from South Tipperary, would endure through the coming struggle.

Robinson had an able adjutant in the figure of Seán Treacy. These two men held long debates and discussions about pushing a more militant policy in their area. Séumas Robinson maintained that Treacy was the only person with whom he ever fully discussed the plan of campaign. Both men were in total agreement that the military approach was now playing second fiddle to the political. Focus, of late, had all been placed on a number of by-elections, the Anti-Conscription Campaign and the 1918 General Election. The impending formation of Dáil Éireann and possible representations to the International Peace Conference in Paris, where the rights of small nations were being pressed, took pre-eminence.

The haemorrhaging of Volunteers was a cause of concern. Treacy is purported to have said something to the effect that if things continue like this 'we will have to shoot someone and make the bloody enemy organise us.' This is the context in which Soloheadbeg was planned. Robinson recalled Treacy informing him about the consignment of gelignite:

> ...there would be from two to six R.I.C. guarding the cart, that they would be armed and that there was the possibility of shooting. "Good", said I, "Go ahead, but under the condition that you let me know in time to be there myself with a couple of men from the local Battalion," men with whom I would go tiger hunting. Then Seán Treacy said "Will you get permission from G.H.Q.?" I looked inquiringly at Seán to see if he were serious, before I replied. "It will be unnecessary so long as we do not ask for their permission. If we ask, we must await their reply." Transport was slow in those early days and it might take so long that the gelignite could easily arrive before permission was received. "Who will take responsibility?" he queried. I said "I will." I have seldom seen anyone look so pleasantly relieved. When Seán was suddenly pleased with anything his quizzical eyes opened for a flash and the tip of his tongue licked the outside corner of his lips.

The Soloheadbeg Ambush would be, in Robinson's own words, the accidental starting point of what became known later as 'The Tan War:'

> I have said 'accidental' because 'providential' might sound a bit presumptuous, tho' in point of fact there is no such thing as an accident not known beforehand to, and not allowed by Providence; and because Volunteers all over the country were as prepared, as anxious and as willing as we to see the ball started rolling and would have started it

in similar circumstances; and we certainly would not have been able to carry on if the Army and the country were not prepared to help us.

Robinson and Treacy realised the possible consequences for them, and indeed the probable consequences if the Army were not prepared to stand behind their action, especially if any casualties were inflicted. Due consideration was given to what they were about to embark upon. Reflecting upon the context and circumstance surrounding the ambush, Robinson documented:

> We did not rush in without thought of the consequences to the about-to-be-set-up Government and the Movement as a whole. I thought long, deeply and anxiously and I almost panicked when I saw the date of the Dáil meeting drawing near and no sign of the gelignite coming. I was most anxious not to compromise the Dáil by starting anything that might be tagged on to them. If we had the ball rolling before the existence of the Dáil had been fully promulgated the British authorities would be pleased to think that Soloheadbeg was the action of irresponsibles and the Dáil would be saved by righteous indignation speeches of dyed-in-the-wood pacifist members. I knew that our Gallican Clergy [those aligned with the British State] would help unconsciously in the delusion that we were pariahs.

Soloheadbeg, in today's parlance, would possibly be described as a well-timed event. Tadgh (Tim) Crowe, a participant in the ambush, recalled that it was probably about the second week in January 1919 that Seán Treacy told him of the intention to seize a consignment of gelignite which was due for delivery at Soloheadbeg quarry. Treacy informed Crowe that he was one of the men selected to carry out the operation. The quarry was operated by the County Council who had it on lease from the owners. Again, it was emphasised that the date on which the gelignite would be delivered from Tipperary military barracks and the strength of the RIC escort which would accompany it were uncertain.

In accordance with Treacy's instructions, Crowe reported to Mrs. Breen's (Dan's mother) cottage at Donohill on 14 January. There he met Breen and Treacy and the three of them went to the 'Tin Hut' at Greenane, which was an unoccupied house on some farmland. They were joined there during the night by Séumas Robinson and Seán Hogan. Maurice Crowe, Patrick McCormack, Paddy O'Dwyer, Michael Ryan, Arthur Barlow and Con Power reported next day. During the days that followed there were changes in the personnel. There were days when Brian Shanahan, Ned O'Reilly, Dinny Lacey and Sean O'Meara were part of the ambush party.

Their plans were relatively simple according to Crowe. Each morning, two of the party left to scout for the coming of the County Council employees and the police escort with the gelignite. The remainder of the party went to the ambush position which was about 150 yards from the entrance to the quarry. There was reasonable cover behind a whitethorn hedge at a place known locally as Cranitch's field. Here was also located a gate that gave easy access to the road.

Wednesday came, then Thursday, Friday too and nothing. The men were stood down for the weekend and resumed their watching brief on Monday morning which again passed with the same routine. The Volunteers returned each evening to the "Tin Hut," lit a fire and spent the night there. In the participants' recollections of their conversations around the fire, there were divergent views as to what the strength of the escort would be. Various suggestions were made about the best method of holding the escort captive after they were disarmed and until the gelignite was safely spirited away. They all assumed that the police would surrender when called upon to halt and put up their hands, and Tadgh Crowe was adamant 'that none of us contemplated that the venture would end in bloodshed and loss of life.' Most participants in their recollections were at odds to stipulate that the deaths of the RIC Constables were not premeditated.

Séumas Robinson similarly recalled that the general instructions which he, as OC, issued had a bearing on the ethics of the ambush. He specified that if only two RIC Constables should accompany the cart they were to be challenged, but if there were six of them, they were to be met with a volley as the cart reached the gate. Robinson was anxious to articulate this and he later outlined that:

> The reason for the difference was that there would be so little danger to us if only two appeared that it would be inhuman not to give them an opportunity of surrendering, but if six police turned up, they, with their rifles, would be too great a danger to the eight of us to take any such risk as to challenge them and thus hand over our initiative. We had only one Winchester Repeater rifle and an agglomeration of small-arms.

Around midday on the Tuesday, 21 January 1919 at roughly the same time Dáil Éireann was meeting for the first time in Dublin, Paddy O'Dwyer cycled back along the Donohill Road from Tipperary, where he had been scouting, with the news that a horse and cart, with the gelignite, had left the Tipperary military barracks. It was accompanied by James Godfrey, driver of the horse and cart and another County Council employee named Patrick Flynn along with two RIC men, Constables O'Connell and McDonnell. The ambush party moved into their prearranged positions. Michael Ryan soon reported that the cart and its escort were approaching.

After long days consisting of boredom and anxious waiting for the gelignite to arrive, the moment was almost upon them. Séumas Robinson recorded:

> Naturally we had already discussed the plan of attack. I had encouraged everyone to give his views in order to size-up his ingenuity, common sense and judgment. The final consensus of their opinion was that we should lie concealed on either side of the gate, rush out with a yell, overawe and overwhelm them the moment the cart reached the gate. In summing up I suggested that I thought that that would resemble "gorilla" warfare rather than guerrilla tactics, that it would betray an unsoldierly lack of discipline and self-control, and would create a false impression of headstrong, headlong hardihood. Then there was the danger of men keyed up with excitement not knowing when to shoot, (orders would not be heard above the din), triggers would be pulled instead of pressed to the grave danger of our own men bunched together and milling around. Then it was suggested that we spread along the hedge with two to do the rushing out at the gate, the rest to cover off the retreat and the advance of the R.I.C. But they all wanted to be one of the two at the gate which warmed my heart because I could see that those "cocks" would fight tho' not one of them had been in a fight under fire before. I insisted that no one should risk life or limb, that all were to remain behind the hedge tho' only two police were reported coming. Seán Treacy and Dan Breen, at the last exciting moment, started to insist that they should be allowed to rush out. Breen seemed to have lost control of himself declaring with grinding teeth and a very high-pitched excited voice that he'd go out and face them. I gave an upward nod of my head which meant "cui bono" [*for whose benefit*], but I made a mental note that that man should never be put in charge of a fight. I did not want any

Balaclava-like heroics, which, as the French Military Attaché declared, "is not war."

There were eight in the ambush party that day: Séumas Robinson, Seán Treacy, Dan Breen, Paddy O'Dwyer, Michael Ryan, Seán Hogan, Patrick McCormack and Tadgh Crowe.

Robinson asked Treacy to remain behind the hedge at the left of the gate where there was a very convenient arm-rest. Treacy had a small-calibre Winchester repeating rifle. Robinson felt that a rifle is comparatively cumbersome in a hold-up situation and should be used to provide cover from a vantage point. He also felt that the hot-headed tension of Breen made it even more vitally important that Treacy should be cool, calm and collected in order to be able to deal with any emergency:

One could depend on cool riflemen. Small arms in the hands of men in their first fight, no matter how cool those men may be, are almost useless at a range of more than two yards. There was nothing for it but to walk over to Seán and say quietly: "Seán you must take that as an order." Seán grimaced and with a little shrug of one shoulder got down on one knee and cocked his rifle "at the ready." The rumbling of the cart was drawing near; I walked quickly the five or six yards to the left where Paddy O'Dwyer was waiting for me. Our job was to spring over the hedge the moment the challenge "hands up" was given, and seize the horse while the R.I.C. were covered. A few yards farther back the R.I.C. had unslung their carbines, but it was clearly just routine. Still, it meant they were ready. The R.I.C. were behind the cart, and, as they appeared opposite the gate, the high-pitched challenge "Hands Up" rang out. Before the first sound had time to re-echo O'Dwyer and I were over the ditch and grabbing the reins. The R.I.C. seemed to be at first amused at the sight of Dan Breen's burly figure with nose and mouth covered with a handkerchief; but with a sweeping glance they saw his revolver and O'Dwyer and me, they could see only three of us. In a flash their rifles were brought up, the bolts worked and triggers pressed two shots rang out, but not from the carbines: the cut-off had been overlooked: The two shots came from Treacy and Tim Crowe. Those shots were the signal for general firing. At the inquest [it was stated] the fatal wounds were "caused by small-calibre bullets."

Paddy O'Dwyer also put on record that 'I distinctly remember seeing one of the R.I.C. men bringing his carbine to the aiming position and working the bolt, and the impression I got was that he was aiming at either Robinson or myself…After the long wait, the whole thing happened very suddenly, in less, perhaps, than half a minute, and in much less time than it takes to relate.' It was clear that Séumas Robinson was in the thick of the action and not a bit player as suggested by Dan Breen in his Witness Statement.

Caught unaware, the RIC men instinctively and in line with their military training, raised their weapons to fire. The safety catches ensured that their efforts were futile but demonstrated that their intent was deadly. With equal deadly intent came the shots from the Volunteers and the two RIC Constables lay dead on the road. The first shots had been fired, and indeed the first causalities had now fallen in what would turn into a renewal of hostilities between the forces of Irish Republicanism and those of the British Empire.

Both Robinson and Treacy viewed the RIC as the glue that held Britain's occupation of Ireland together. Their presence was visible in every parish across the country with a network of barracks that ensured they were the eyes and ears in every locality. They felt that, as a police force, their focus was not on 'ordinary' crime but rather on ensuring that everything national was monitored and, if needed, suppressed and that purpose was part of their 'conditioning' during training in the Phoenix Park Depot. The force was armed, and there was a long history of animosity and distrust of 'Peelers' in Tipperary. They were seen as obtrusive spies who had evicted people from their farms during the 'Land War' and suppressed previous rebellions, earning the title 'Royal' as a reward for their loyal endeavours. Robinson and Treacy concluded that if any war of national liberation was to be successful, then the RIC needed to be rendered ineffective. They were to be systematically targeted and boycotted. This emphasis on combatting the RIC would yield results that were not achieved in past insurgencies.

The dead policemen were stripped of their weapons and equipment as the Volunteers made haste to make their escape. Paddy O'Dwyer recalled that:

> Michael Ryan and Paddy McCormack remained on the road with Séumas Robinson guarding Godfrey and Flynn until such time as the gelignite was a safe distance away. Tadhg Crowe and I took the two carbines with us and hid them at a spot on the railway line about half a mile from the scene of the ambush and where it was convenient for Tadhg to collect them later. We then parted and I went home to Hollyford on foot.

Seán Treacy had made all the arrangements for dumping the gelignite in a secure location. Dan Breen and Seán Hogan mounted the cart. Breen, standing up with the reins, whipped the horse and away they went at frenzied speed along the bumpy road.

A new danger sprung up in the aftermath of the ambush. Being January, the weather was extremely cold. It was assumed that

Dan Breen, who had worked on the railway, would have known the danger of jolting gelignite that was frozen and would have exercised care. Hogan relayed afterwards that he tried to caution Breen but either he couldn't hear him or he put no "seem" in it. The cart had been brought from the town at a snail's pace with the driver leading the horse by the head. It was now being ferried away at speed.

The gelignite was brought to local IRA activist, Tom Carew. He hid the explosives so well that they were never discovered although every inch of ground was searched and poked for miles around, including the actual place where the gelignite was dumped.

It had been arranged beforehand that Treacy, Breen and Hogan should meet and go 'on-the-run' and stay at a 'safe house' belonging to Mrs. Tobin of Tincurry. This arrangement became even more prudent given that the two RIC men were dead, Séumas Robinson would now join them. Large scale search operations followed. The raids and searches became so intense that the locals soon called Robinson, Treacy, Breen and Hogan 'The Big Four.'

Robinson went to Kilshenane to tie up some loose ends and to ascertain what the reactions to the ambush were. According to Robinson, Mrs. Cussin, Éamon Ó Duibhir's sister, 'was very perturbed; she asked: "Séumas, how will you go to Confession." I replied, "Mrs. Cussin, when I go to Confession, I go to confess my sins not to boast of my virtues!" "Oh, that's all right then" she said, brightening up, and proceeded with her preparations for a great feed which was the first I had had for nearly a week.' Clearly his conscious was clear about what had just transpired:

I had no intention of staying in Kilshenane, that night as the R.I.C. knew that I was the O/C. of the Brigade because they always called on me (tho' I was supposed to be only a farmhand on Eamon Uí Duibhir's place) whenever anything of a military nature occurred in the district as when Jimmy Leahy, O/C. Mid. Tipp. Brigade and some of his men coming from an aireacht, broke some pillar-boxes in Dundrum, the R.I.C. visited me first. Jimmy Brown and I were in the garden. I picked up a fork as I went to meet them followed by Jimmy Brown. The Sergeant was indignant that I picked up the fork. He asked me why. I told him that I wasn't going to be arrested alive again. He said they were not there to arrest me; there had been some damage done to pillar-boxes in Dundrum and H.Q. (R.I.C.) had to have a report on my comments. "Why to me?" "Well, to whom else would we come?"

Robinson asked Jimmy Brown to brush the mud off the trousers he had worn at the ambush. He then left Kilshenane with Jimmy promising to do the needful. Séumas had warned that the police would be along at any moment. According to Robinson, Jimmy didn't get time to brush down the trousers during that exciting day:

It was about 12 midnight when he [Jimmy] started to clean the trousers. After about ten minutes he turned them inside-out, as "half the mud of the Soloheadbeg quarry must have been on them." He threw the trousers over the end of his bed and started to undress. Jimmy hadn't time to get into bed when the police arrived looking for me. Jack Cussin, Éamon's brother-in-law, was in bed but he got up and dressed quickly before the police got in. Finding his bed warm they concluded that I had just escaped. They searched every corner, nook and cranny for any tell-tale evidence, but none was found. Jimmy Brown told me afterwards with chuckles how the R.I.C. pitched the trousers from one place to another as it got in the way of their search. Those trousers were new and looked very innocent with the clean inside out.

When the news of the ambush reached Dublin there were vehement condemnations from both the political and military components of the Republican Movement, something which Séumas Robinson would never forget and would be partly responsible for the strained future relations between the Dublin based national leadership and South Tipperary. Robinson remembered in particular that his friend from prison and one-time host in Dublin Arthur Griffith said something along the lines of:

> ...if that sort of thing were allowed to continue, we would soon be eating one another. Arthur Griffith was possibly (to him probably) expecting the suppression of the Dáil would follow, and his life's work thrown back a quarter of a century. Others too were equally shocked, the clergy in particular or those of them who were unconsciously (I hope) influenced by Maynooth Jansenism or Gallicanism and or had blood relationship with the British Forces, especially the R.I.C. - those Irish Janissaries.

From pulpits all over Ireland the condemnation was fierce with one local priest declaring that he hoped Ireland would not follow where Tipperary had led with this 'deed of blood.'

Two days after leaving Kilshenane, Mick Davern accompanied Robinson to Glenough where they met a number of Volunteers from Mid-Tipperary who then brought them to where Treacy, Hogan and Breen were staying. The hunt was on to capture them, and large parties of RIC and British military were combing the area. The meticulously built up Brigade infrastructure was invoked to shelter and move them around, but not everyone was willing to shelter the Soloheadbeg men. It was evident that the area was not yet conditioned for armed confrontation and its ramifications.

As soon as Robinson walked in the door of the safe house, Seán Treacy, wearing his whimsical smile, handed him a dispatch from GHQ. The two Officers were summoned to Dublin to account for their actions. The next morning Robinson and Treacy set off on bicycles for the city, leaving Dan Breen and Seán Hogan behind. They stopped at a house in Carlow. Séumas Robinson was always amazed that Seán Treacy seemed to be known and liked everywhere. After staying the night, they again set off for their rendezvous in the city.

Kathleen Boland, the sister of prominent Republican Harry, remembered the circumstances of Robinson and Treacy's arrival in Dublin. She, along with a network of her comrades in Cumann na mBan, would become a staunch support network for the Tipperary Volunteers when they were in the capital:

> Joe O'Reilly came to our shop in 64 Middle Abbey Street. I should have mentioned that Harry opened a tailoring and outfitting business about October of 1917, and it became an important centre for dispatches from all places, especially from Cork, Kerry and Tipperary. Joe said Mick Collins wanted to see me. I went to his office in Mary Street, just near Liffey Street. He said there were some very important men from Tipperary coming up to Dublin and he was going to send some of them out to me. He also asked me whether I knew any other safe houses where the people were not talkative and where these men could stay under assumed names. I sent Joe O'Reilly to Miss Eva O'Doherty, a quiet girl that I knew in Cumann na mBan, to get some safe houses, and she recommended to him Malone's house in Grantham Street and the Delaney's in Heytesbury Street. That evening, Séumas Robinson and

Seán Treacy arrived at our house. I'll never forget my feelings when I saw the condition they were in. The soles were gone from their boots and they were footsore, weary, wet through and hungry. We gave them a hot meal in the kitchen. They stayed with us a couple of nights and then moved on somewhere else. Seán Treacy, Séumas Robinson and their two companions came often to stay with us afterwards, bringing with them various Volunteers.

Now, through Kathleen Boland, 'The Big Four' had a number of safe and secure houses in Dublin where they could seek shelter. Incidentally, Séumas Robinson would later marry Brigid Keating from Heytesbury Street and Dan Breen would marry one of the Malone girls from Grantham Street.

On arrival in Dublin, word was sent to GHQ, and almost immediately they received a dispatch giving instructions where to meet Michael Collins. However, Collins was waiting for them on the street with his notebook out. Robinson recalled:

This meeting which was in the street instead of in an office was the first indication we had that we (The Big Four?) were not exactly persona non-grata, at best we were decidedly not warmly welcome in any H.Q. office, except in Peadar Clancy's shop in Talbot Street where we were always received hilariously. They were rightly afraid of our blazing trail being followed by spies. Mick seemed to be keeping his eyes peeled watching everyone in the street without moving his head. His glance would come back to us. He greeted us with: "Well, everything is fixed-up; be ready to go in a day or two." "To go where?" I asked. "To the States" he said. "Why?" "Well, isn't it the usual thing to do after!" "We don't want to go to the States or anywhere else." "Well," said Mick "a great many people seem to think it is the only thing to do." I began to be afraid that G.H.Q.

had begun to give way to Sinn Féin pacifism, and with a little acerbity I said: "Look here, to kill a couple of policemen for the country's sake and leave it at that by running away would be so wanton as to approximate too closely to murder." "Then what do you propose to do?" "Fight it out of course." Mick Collins, without having shown the slightest emotion during this short interview, now suddenly closed his notebook with a snap saying as he strode off with the faintest of faint smiles on his lips but with a big laugh in his eyes: "That's all right with me."

Treacy was bitterly disappointed with this response and he expected a more enthusiastic welcome in Dublin. According to Robinson he touched Treacy on the shoulder and said: "'Come on Seán, that's great!" He said "What's great?"' I responded, "Well, I expected only tacit recognition. G.H.Q. naturally want to sit comfortably in their armchairs organising until they can see the daylight ahead. If we can blaze the trail, they will then encourage the rest of the country to do the same.'" Robinson felt that 'Seán Treacy didn't see the laugh in Mick Collins' eyes and that, coupled with Mick's abruptness (despite his "That's all right with me") made him still think that G.H.Q. regarded us as at best a nuisance.' Robinson would have known Collins much better than Treacy, having come in contact with him through their mutual connection to the Plunkett family, the 1916 Rising and subsequent imprisonment.

Robinson and Treacy returned to Tipperary to pick up their harried and hunted life on-the-run. Despite the dangers, their comrades and a small corps of sympathisers ensured that they had protection and shelter. Life on-the-run was indeed harsh, especially with the weather being freezing cold. They had irregular sleep and meals, were soaked on a consistent basis, but they were now, in essence, full-time soldiers. They were able to go throughout the command area, and further afield, encouraging the adoption of a more militant policy among the Volunteers. The British military and RIC were also causing resentment in the area due to their widespread raids and search operations. This activity was turning an initial circumspect response to the ambush into a more sympathetic one.

Looking back at that particular period Robinson recorded:

> Seán Treacy had a genius for organisation and making friends. We were kept busy going around the Brigade Area contacting officers and trying to get things going. We were being searched for daily. From two to five thousand soldiers would concentrate on an area, search every house and field rounding up all the male population of military age and always we were just outside one of the apices of the triangle, with field glasses enjoying the sight. We had to get men in every Company Area to be ready to scout for us, and to do it armed and be prepared to join us if attacked. Soon we began to be envied, the men wanting to be with us all the time. The Volunteers were told to go 'on-the-run' rather than lose liberty or their arms, and to be ready to fight for both.

The reaction by the British authorities to the shooting of the two RIC Constables assisted in organising the South Tipperary Brigade into an active military unit. As a general state of war did not exist at this stage, the troop movements went largely unhindered, but the Volunteers were active to ensure that the 'Big Four' were safe. Robinson noted the tactics being deployed by the British; these observations, coupled with his evolving intelligence apparatus and Brigade infrastructure, would ensure they would avoid capture. He recounted:

> A Captain and two Lieutenants set out with 100 N.C.Os. and men from Templemore across country to the borders

of South Tipperary at Boherlahan. They arrived fairly late in the day and immediately camped on both sides of the bridge across the Suir. They had not been reported, they had travelled so secretly, and in their camp, they were well concealed. They left the bridge clear. No one was challenged from the side he started from (he could see nothing) but when he reached the other side he was challenged and held up. From a distance no one could see a soldier. They were highly trained and knew their business! About 5a.m. next morning a Volunteer on horseback crossed the bridge and was held up and searched... they searched him more thoroughly again and found nothing until one of the soldiers noticed something on the sole of a boot. They prised open the sole and discovered a dispatch. But what a dispatch! There can be little doubt that the Captain had been well warned about our wonderful Intelligence system. He was so careful to play safe that he didn't let his Lieutenants know where he intended to go until they were ready to march each morning... The Captain kept his intended itinerary to himself concealed in a diary which he kept in a pocket inside his tunic. When he read the dispatch that poor Captain was not only mystified, he panicked for he left at once on a forced march to Clonmel. Why? Because of what he saw in the captured dispatch. He read: "To O/C. Capt, and two Lts. With 100 N.C.Os and men set out from Templemore on the morning of... He encamped at ... Next morning the Column left under sealed orders and arrived at ... They are now camped on the south side of the Suir at Boherlahan holding both bridgeheads, concealed. They have seen no I.R.A." This was splendid intelligence work surely by an invisible enemy. They had not only noted his every movement but had got his name (and who knows perhaps the names and addresses of them all). This was disconcerting enough but when he read further his hair must have stood on end: "He intends to go from here to … then to …" and right to the end of his secret itinerary. It was too much for the poor Captain. Clever ordinary military intelligence is bad enough to have to contend with (and he had seen for himself how perfect our intelligence was) but this clairvoyance was diabolical; the utterly impossible was not impossible to I.R.A. Intelligence.

The perhaps surprising source for this vital piece of intelligence was Mrs de Vere Hunt. Described by Robinson as a 'tall stately lady.' She was a member of the Anglo-Irish gentry and was viewed, by merit of her background, as being unionist in the locality by Republicans and British Military alike. Indeed, some IRA officers deemed the family as being a danger so they wanted to drive them from the locality. Séumas Robinson intervened, stating that this action would be anti-Republican in nature and that they should try to win over people like her rather than alienate them from the cause of Irish Independence. This intervention by Robinson was deeply appreciated by Mrs de Vere Hunt, who, unbeknown to most, became a staunch and reliable supporter.

The British Military stopped for the night at the Hunt homestead. Mrs. de Vere Hunt told Séumas Robinson afterwards that 'she approached the Captain and bade them "welcome in these dreadful days." She then invited him and his Lieutenants have dinner with her. The Captain agreed with alacrity. Mrs. Hunt gave her maid the evening off "because maids are dangerous to have around at times like this, they talk so much!" This gave her the excuse to do the serving herself.' They enjoyed the meal and when it was over the Captain dismissed his two Lieutenants and settled down to peruse his diary while Mrs. de Vere Hunt busied herself clearing the table and chatting, keeping on the move.

Continuing the account, Robinson recorded:

> The Captain's back was mostly towards her. She is a very tall lady and her sight must have been astonishingly keen and she must have had a photographic memory, for, as he turned the leaves slowly, she managed to steal a glance at each and memorised the gist of it. She had the dispatch ready in no time and had it sent to the local officer.

By February 1919, the RIC were increasingly frustrated that none of 'The Big Four' had been captured. There were reports of torturing civilians, including Seán Hogan's younger brother who was abducted and interrogated. The British Government proceeded to proclaim Martial Law on Tipperary. Fairs, markets and public gatherings were prohibited. The civilian population became further alienated, and their sympathy for the men on-the-run was growing all the time.

Séumas Robinson felt that nothing remained but to hit back. He produced the following proclamation, which he was prepared to sign, making South Tipperary a special military area in the name of the Irish Republic. He sent the draft to GHQ for approval:

PROCLAMATION.

Whereas a foreign and tyrannical Government is preventing Irishmen exercising the civil right of buying and selling in their own markets in their own country,

And
Whereas almost every Irishman who has suffered the death penalty for Ireland was sentenced to death solely on the strength of the evidence and reports of policemen who, therefore, are dangerous spies,

And

Whereas thousands of Irishmen have been deported and sentenced solely on the evidence of these same hirelings, assassins and traitorous spies the police,

And

Whereas the life, limb and living of no citizen of Ireland is safe while these paid spies are allowed to infest the country,

And

Whereas it has come to our knowledge that some men and boys have been arrested and drugged,

And

Whereas there are a few Irishmen who have sunk to such depths of degradation that they are prepared to give information about their neighbours and fellow countrymen to the police,

And

Whereas all these evils will continue as long as the people permit:

We hereby proclaim the South Riding of Tipperary a military area with the following regulations:

(a) A policeman found within the said area on and after the _____ day of February 1919, will be deemed to have forfeited his life. The more notorious police being dealt with, as far as possible, first.

(b) On and after the _____ day of February 1919, every person in the pay of England (magistrates, jurors etc.) who helps England to rule this country or who assists in any way the upholders of foreign Government in this South Riding of Tipperary will be deemed to have forfeited his life.

(c) Civilians who give information to the police or soldiery, especially such information as is of a serious character, if convicted, will be executed, i.e. shot or hanged.

(d) Police, doctors, prison officials who assist at or who countenance or who are responsible for, or in any way connected with the drugging of an Irish citizen for the purpose of obtaining information, will be deemed to have forfeited his life and may be hanged or drowned or shot at sight as a common outlaw. Offending parties will be executed should it take years to track them down.

(e) Every citizen must assist when required in enabling us to perform our duty.

By Order: Séumas MacRóibín

The reply came back from GHQ to Robinson stating 'That proclamation must not be published!' Robinson didn't think at that time Headquarters would have baulked at what the Proclamation implied and he lost confidence in GHQ's desire for 'vaunted ruthless warfare.' Their words did not match the Tipperary Brigade's deeds. A mutual sense of animosity began to develop further between GHQ and South Tipperary.

Séumas Robinson, outlined with a hint of resentment:

There were about seven of us Volunteers 'on-the-run' for our lives in South Tipperary at that time. We were on the alert 24 hours in the day, while the R.I.C. were able to move about with impunity, lording it over all the people, manhandling them, arresting them, questioning them, searching them, raiding their houses, allowed to move around freely day and night. In those early days our young blood would boil at "caution" which we then regarded as "the better part of cowardice." We began to think that G.H.Q., situated in Dublin which was very quiet indeed at that time (February 1919), had little notion of what we of the Southern Counties were up against. In fact, G.H.Q. never did get any practical first-hand experience of the fight in either the City or the country. Not a single member of the G.H.Q. staff ever came down the country to see things for himself. They depended entirely on reports of local officers, and, later, on reports of H.Q. Organisers who were trained in the City on Regular Army military manuals. The best of these by far, Ernie O'Malley, wasn't a week with us when he realised the difference between organisation on paper and on the field, that guerrillas and guerrilla tactics and training were nearly as far apart as the poles from Regulars and their "orders are orders" training. Regulars are trained to be hidebound automatons, while it is necessary for Volunteers to be trained as autonomous freelancers.

Robinson had called a Brigade Staff meeting in anticipation of their Proclamation being approved. He even went as far as getting copies printed for distribution. The response of GHQ was thus conveyed to the assembled men and disappointment reigned. Séumas Robinson then said with significant deliberation:

"As H.Q. has forbidden me to post up this Proclamation, I hereby warn you all that if I see anyone pasting up one of these posters on telegraph poles, trunks of trees, walls or on the gable-ends of R.I.C. barracks or doors or windows, and especially if I see you pinning one on to the tail of a Bobby's coat you will be severely punished!" They took me literally at my word: I never saw a more enthusiastic scramble to get those papers out of my sight. In spite (?) of my warning they were posted all over South Tipperary and a bit farther away too.

The militant mood of South Tipperary was certainly increasing. The 'premier coup' was now done. Soloheadbeg had created the circumstances where the push towards guerrilla warfare was almost unavoidable; soon another incident involving 'The Big Four' would make it inevitable.

An aerial photograph showing industrial land around Clonard. Included is Sevastopol Street, bottom right, where Séumas Robinson was born. Also visible is Ross's Mill.

Benares Street in the Clonard area. The Robinson family lived here before they moved to Glasgow in 1903.

The Belfast 1798 Centenary Parade on the Falls Road pictured at the bottom of Clonard Street. As a young boy Séumas Robinson participated in the parade.

A member of the first Fianna Éireann pictured in 1902. Joe and Séumas Robinson were members of this prototype Republican youth organsiation.

Joe Robinson: IRB member, Fianna Éireann organiser, Captain in the Irish Volunteers and prolific gunrunner. He had a huge influence on his younger brother.

Pictured in the 1950s is Robson Street, Glasgow, where the
Robinson family lived.

The Glasgow Fianna: tried and trusted, Joe Robinson utilised their services in the quest for arms and explosives.

Irish Volunteers (Company A) Glasgow

SECOND MONTHLY

LECTURE and CONCERT

Sunday First, October 3rd,

VOLUNTEER HALL, 34 Ann St. (City),

Off Jamaica Street.

National Programme—Songs and Readings.

Those in Sympathy Cordially Invited.

Advertisement for a concert in aid of 'A' Company, Glasgow Irish Volunteers. This unit was commanded by Joe Robinson.

Hopkins' Corner at O'Connell Bridge, where Séumas Robinson was stationed for part of Easter Week until the building was destroyed.

A photograph showing the complete destruction of Hopkins' Corner and damage along Eden Quay at the end of Easter Week.

An injured James Connolly, on the stretcher, during the surrender at the end of Easter Week. Connolly inspired Robinson during the Rising and would influence him for the rest of his life.

A group photo of prisoners in Stafford Gaol, possibly including Séumas Robinson sitting front row sixth from right.

MR. WALLER

EVADERS OF MILITARY SERVICE

1545	CARMICHAEL, Andrew	Says he was born in Glasgow, address unknown. Joined I.V. 2 years ago, went to Dublin to take part in rising.
1150	COUGHLAN, Joseph	London. Letter from this prisoner to Miss Coughlan c/o Miss M. Smyth 1, Aquila St., St. John's Wood, N.W.
1543	FRIEL, Bernard	Glasgow. Exact address unknown. Aged 20. Says he worked 5 years for William Weare & Co., Glasgow.
1547	SUPPLE, Patrick	Lived with his parents in Liverpool until Jan. 1916. Exact address unknown.
1501	KERR, Neill	6, Florida St., Strand Rd., Liverpool.
1161	KING, George	Says he came from Wexford City. Committee think he may have come from Gt. Britain. Police say possibly from provinces of Ireland or Gt. Britain. Only address known is Larkfield, Kimmage.
1587	KING. Patrick	Brother of above, and same remarks apply, though known to have been shipping clerk in Liverpool some months ago. Went thence to Wexford.
1209	LUNDY. Jas.	Was employed in Liverpool but left at the end of Jan. 1916. Parents in Liverpool. No further address.
1186	MURPHY, Ml.	Worked in London last year and lived at Salesian School, Battersea, S.W.
1477	O'LEARY, Joseph D.	11, Tremadoc Rd., Clapham, S.W.
1204	O'REILLY, Joseph	Sorter G.P.O. London. Refused to join Army and services dispensed with. Subsequently worked as a "putee" but where unknown, but it was not in Bantry, to which place he returned early in 1916. He is a weaver.
1112	ROBINSON, James	Home adress: 10, Robson St., Govan Hill, Glasgow. He was for 2 years before the rising employed as a painter in Edinburgh. Neither the address of his employers nor his lodging in Edinburgh is known. He refused to join the Army and his employer dispensed with his services.
25	VIZE, Joseph	34, Greenhead Lane, Govan, Glasgow.

A list of 'Evaders' compiled by Prison Authorities of men with addresses in Britain who they would try to conscript into the British Army. Included is Séumas Robinson, second from bottom.

An RIC report from early 1918 detailing that Éamon Ó
Duibhir and Séumas Robinson were making 'Seditious
speeches and drilling in uniforms of a military character.'

Séumas Robinson, listed at top of page, in the Prison
Register of Cork Gaol where he was remanded for Drilling
in 1918.

THE BELFAST PRISON UPROAR

Extensive Damage Done by Sinn Feiners.

MOCK RECRUITING MEETINGS HELD

The situation in connection with the revolt of the Sinn Fein prisoners in Belfast Jail was practically unchanged yesterday, and the state of siege continues. It is understood that the Sinn Feiners have provisions in hand which will enable them to hold out until about Thursday. The authorities have cut off the supply of water, gas, and electric light to the wing occupied by the prisoners, and this step will probably deprive the prisoners of the means of cooking the food which they have in store. It is known, however, that they have candles.

A band has been improvised by the prisoners, and musical selections are the order of the day, while night has been rendered hideous to the residents of the streets in the vicinity of the jail. "The Soldier's Song" is roared at intervals, and one of the hospital "patients" gave "The Rising of the Moon" by way of variety. It is stated that when music has ceased to charm the Sinn Feiners amuse themselves by holding mock recruiting meetings

A press report detailing incidents in Belfast Prison. Séumas Robinson was serving a sentence for Drilling at the time of the 'Mutiny' in 1918.

Republican Prisoners on the roof of Belfast Prison during the 1918 'Mutiny.'

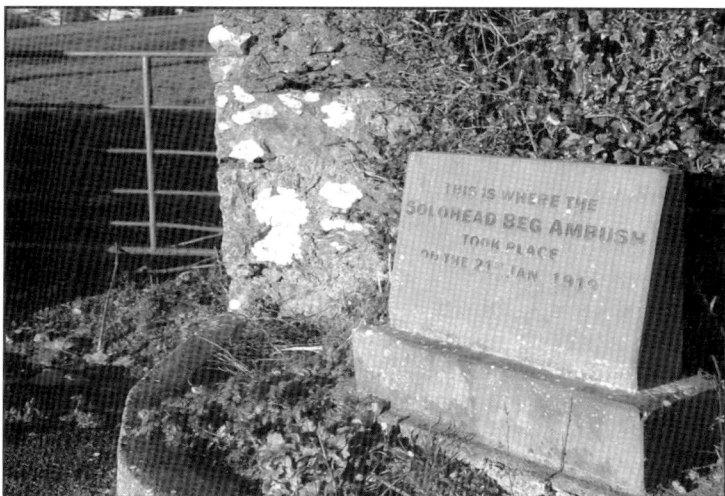

The gate close to Soloheadbeg Quarry where the ambush occurred on 21 January 1919.

An offer of reward after the Soloheadbeg Ambush. This bounty was never claimed.

Séumas Robinson, Seán Treacy, Dan Breen and Michael Brennan pictured in County Clare, 1919.

The Railway Station at Knocklong.

Seán Hogan, who was rescued at Knocklong Station.

Detectives of G Division. 'The Big Four' took part in the early attacks on the political detectives as part of the intelligence war directed by Michael Collins.

A British soldier points to a bullet hole in Lord French's Car after the ambush at Ashtown, Dublin, in December 1919. 'The Big Four' participated in this attack.

Hollyford RIC Barrack, pictured in the background, was attacked by the IRA in May 1920. Séumas Robinson and Ernie O'Malley played particularly hazardous roles igniting the roof of the building.

Séumas Robinson pictured in Tipperary, 1921.

Members of the Third Tipperary Brigade IRA pictured in 1921.

Munster T.D. Married.—The marriage took place on December 20 in University Church, St. Stephen's Green, of Comdt. Seamus Robinson, T.D, for Waterford and East Tipperary, son of Mr. James Robinson, Tipperary, with Miss Brigid Keating, daughter of Mr. Patrick Keating, 71 Heytesbury street, Dublin. Miss Annie Keating, sister of the bride, was bridesmaid, and Comdt. Donal Breen, best man. The officiating clergy were the Rev. E. R. McCarthy, Tipperary, assisted by the Rev. J. P. Sherwin, University Church; Rev. C. E. Murphy, St. Kevin's, and Rev. Fr. O'Callaghan. A brother of the bridegroom, Mr. Joseph Robinson, is at present suffering imprisoment for an alleged attempt to import explosives into Ireland.

Wedding announcement in the press of Séumas Robinson's marriage to Brigid Keating, December 1921.

Séumas Robinson and Brigid Keating's Wedding in Dublin,
December 1921.

Séumas Robinson and Liam Mellows waiting on an arms shipment for the Anti-Treaty IRA at Helvick Head, County Waterford, 1922.

An attack on the Four Courts, Dublin, in June 1922 by the
Free State Army signalled the commencement of Civil War.

Members of the Anti-Treaty IRA pictured in 1922 at
Divisional Headquarters, Clonmel.

ROBINSON. James.   Kilsheenane House, Cashel, Co. Tipperary.
                   and c/o J. Delaney, 71, Heytesbury St., Dublin.
                   Dundrum, Co. Tipperary

Description:- Height 5'1". Sallow complexion. Medium make.
               A Scotchman.

Age, 36 - 40.

ELECTED SINN FEIN M.P. FOR TIPPERARY EAST, MAY 1921.

G.O.C. 2nd Southern Division.   (IX/0661).

Old Black List No. 872.

Member IRB.

~~Was~~ Commandant 3rd South Tipperary Brigade, I.R.A. and formerly
V/Commandant 2nd Dundrum Battalion. (Rev. O.of B. April 1921).

Signs documents as Seamus McR.

Came to Ireland about eight years ago and settled in the house of
a notorious Sinn Feiner, Ed O'Dwyer (Kate) at Kilsheenane, Dundrum
since destroyed as an Official reprisal.

Convicted on several occasions of unlawful assembly.

Implicated with Daniel BREEN in the first murders of Police at
Solshead in January 1919.

Organised numerous outrages and ambushes. (6th Div. B.L. No.2.).
Believed to be the Ringleader in bringing Gelignite into Clonmelly district.
Delegate to I.R.A. Convention at Dublin in January 1920.

Signature in An t'Oglac Book 15-1-19; acted as Drill Instructor
in various parts of Tipperary. (Mulcahy's papers).

Active in obtaining munitions.

Interned on two occasions.   Dangerous character.

Extract from "Irish Bulletin" Vol.5. No.20. dated 29-6-21. "Imprisoned 1916. "Wanted"

Wrote a letter to his mother regretting stoppages of fighting and
expressing willingness to start again if necessary. (I.F.2/5/25(66)

Has been "on the run" since January 1919 and not seen locally since
the Truce began, July 11th 1921.
Held a conference of Bn Comdts in August 1921 8/18/8H9/6
Voted against Ratification of Treaty on Saturday, 7th January 1922.

Reliably reported to be considered by the Provisional Government
as "hopeless and mad" and in consequence difficulty has been experienced in controlling his Division (2nd Southern Division I.R.A.).
Was warned by Provisional Government Military Authorities that unless his Division came into line all Officers would be cashiered
and would become outlaws.   LLHQ. 3.II.22.

Elected on Executive at I.R.A. Convention held in Mansion
House, Dublin, on 26-3-22. (Vide 'Freeman's Journal' 29-3-22.)
Was present at Mansion House Dublin 16.5.22 at a conference
of Army Officers (Republican & Pro) (Irish Independent 17.5.22)
Commands No 3 Tipperary Bde (RT) (Freeman's Journal 273.22)

Part of a British Intelligence Services file summarising
Robinson's involvement in the Irish Revolution through to
the Civil War period.

POBLACHT NA H-EIREANN

PROCLAMATION

WHEREAS: The Irish Republican Army was established to maintain the Irish Republic, and, having sworn allegiance to the Republic, is determined to resist every power, foreign and domestic, inimical thereto; and

WHEREAS: The setting up of the Free State Government is inimical to the established Republic, and the majority in the Dail having connived at the creation of the Free State Government, have by that act forfeited the allegiance of all citizens of the Republic, soldiers and civilians alike; and

WHEREAS: The present Dail Cabinet and the majority of General Headquarters Staff are avowed supporters of the "Articles of Agreement for a Treaty" signed in London on December 6th, 1921, and are using the Army which is the mainstay of the Republic to protect the Provisional Government which is determined to subvert the Republic; and

WHEREAS a disloyal Irish Press is being inspired by those subverters of the Republic to represent the Army and the Nation as having approved of the Articles of Agreement;

NOW, THEREFORE: We, the undersigned having no other means of informing the peoples of other nations that the surrender of the Republic has not been and will not be sanctioned by the people of Ireland and that the people of Ireland will frustrate any attempt to set up any form of government incompatible with absolute Independence and not deriving its authority from the freely expressed will of the Irish people;

AND that the Irish people regard the proposed establishment of the Free State as incompatible with the absolute Independence of Ireland, as the authority by which the Free State is being created is foreign authority;

TAKE this opportunity of giving that information to the world by solemn proclamation;

AND WE do further pledge ourselves to rouse the nation from its lethargy and to band together the Army and the People to resist the treacherous inclusion of Ireland among the British possessions;

AND WE recall to the mind of Irishmen that at Easter Week, 1916, a minority saved the nation from the deceptions of their political leaders and their dishonest press and proclaimed the Independence of Ireland;

AND WE do now call upon the nation in the same manner and to the same glorious end, convinced that a beginning must be made somewhere, some time, and by some one," and that this heroic generation of Irishmen and women need but to know that their independent nationhood is in danger in order to offer every noble service to protect it.

AND WE DO NOW PUBLISH AND PROCLAIM

1. That the attempt to set up the Government of the Free State is illegal and immoral;

2. That the present Dail Cabinet and the majority of General Headquarters Staff, by conniving at the establishment of this illegal Government, have made themselves usurpers with no power but that of tyrants and of traitors;

3. That, therefore, all their orders, decrees and acts have no binding force on the people of the South Tipperary Brigade area, or of any other part of Ireland, and as such are to be resisted by every citizen of the Republic living in this area by every means in his power.

And we do call upon every other unit of the Army to take similar action, and by that means to unite the nation to defeat these domestic enemies who would usurp the national authority and destroy the Independence of Ireland.

We urge upon the nation to save the still unsullied honour of this great Gaelic people by refusing to sell their nationhood for the shameful gains of a false peace and a disgraceful prosperity.

Signed on behalf of the Council of South Tipperary Brigade,

SEAMUS ROBINSON, O.C.	South Tipperary	Brigade
DENIS LACEY, Vice-Cdt.	"	"
SEAN FITZPATRICK, Adjt.	"	"
MICHAEL SHEEHAN, Q.M.	"	"
JEROME DAVIN, O.C. Bn. 1	"	"
PATRICK RYAN, O.C. Bn. 2	"	"
TADG O'DWYER, O.C. Bn. 3	"	"
BRIAN SHANAHAN, O.C. Bn. 4	"	"
PATRICK DALTON, O.C. Bn. 5	"	"
SEAN PRENDERGAST, O.C. Bn. 6	"	"
SEAN WALSH, O.C. Bn. 7	"	"
SEAMUS GILMARTIN, O.C. Bn. 8	"	"

A proclamation issued by the Third Tipperary Brigade, IRA, repudiating The Treaty and Free State Provisional Government.

Survivors of the Knocklong Rescue at a reunion event.
Robinson only attended after a direct appeal from de Valera.
Pictured, from left, are Breen, de Valera, Robinson,
JJ O'Brien, Hogan and Ned O'Brien.

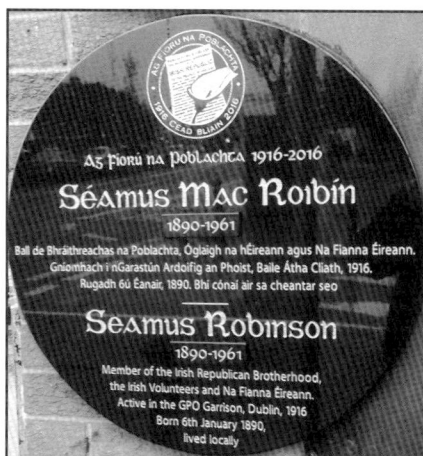

A Plaque dedicated to Séumas Robinson erected in 2016 at
Sevastopol Street, Belfast, to mark the 100th Anniversary of
the Easter Rising.

Commandant General
Seumas Robinson

A photo of an older Séumas Robinson used for his obituary in the *Irish Press*, December 1961.

CHAPTER FIVE

AUTONOMOUS FREELANCERS

The Follow Through: The Rescue at Knocklong May 1919

The hunt for 'The Big Four' continued. They were constantly harried but always remained one step ahead of their pursuers. This was a tough existence, but homes across Tipperary, Limerick and Clare were open to them. Their plight helped gel the Volunteer Organisation together and also harnessed the symbiotic relationship with the local population.

Despite being constantly on-the-run, the business of getting the Volunteer Organisation on a war footing continued. Séumas Robinson reported that:

> Seán Treacy's flair for organisation was only one outlet for his enthusiasm and like Michael Collins (at least in this) he liked to have a finger in the pie of every department. He acted as Adjutant to me sending out Orders as well as his own department of Vice-Commandant. Dan Breen had been elected Quartermaster, but Seán seized every opportunity to buy arms or ammunition and sell them to the Volunteers.

Treacy had acquired some small arms from Peadar Clancy in Dublin as he had been asked by Mick Davern to get him a revolver. Robinson and Treacy went to Kilshenane to see Davern and Éamon Ó Duibhir. When the need arose, Ó Duibhir was always prepared and willing to assist in getting financial help. By all accounts, Seán Treacy dearly loved a chat with anyone who was interesting and likeminded so wanted to spend the night in Kilshenane, but Mick Davern wouldn't hear of it. He knew his Battalion area and his local RIC too well. "'It would be far too dangerous to stay any length of time in Kilshenane, and madness to sleep there.'" A compromise was reached by sleeping just across the road in the house belonging to sympathisers, the O'Brien family.

Next morning, just after the Volunteer guards were dismissed, four RIC men arrived at the O'Brien's house. Robinson and Treacy were in the dining room having breakfast and were totally unaware of the presence of the Constables until they had gone. Mick Davern had arrived with a pitchfork ready to join in the fray. He had crept up close to a Constable who was on guard in front of the house:

> Mick was a very puzzled young man when he saw the R.I.C. coming out and going off quite unruffled. He rushed in to find out the explanation of the mystery. They were only looking for the dog license. When Mrs O'Brien and Mick Davern started talking excitedly, we walked out of the dining room to find out what was the excitement about. "Wouldn't it have been awful, Mick" said she "if the police had leaned, against the door, it would have opened" - this is in reference to the dining room door - the lock was worn and flimsy. "Mam" said Seán Treacy, "a couple of buckets of hot water would clear away all the bloodstains."

The previous day Seán Treacy had shown Mick Davern a .45 revolver and offered it for the price of £6. Davern knew that the Company had no funds but he was to organise a dance in Ballagh for the coming Sunday night for the purpose of raising the required amount for the weapon. He invited 'The Big Four' to attend, which they readily accepted, a decision that would have fatal consequences.

It meant a long stay in one Battalion area, and Treacy thought that would be too long. Robinson felt they were as safe as they could be in the Kilnamanagh Battalion, and it was the first visit he had been able to pay his old Company and Battalion since Soloheadbeg.

The 'Big Four' stayed, and their presence no doubt added to the success of the dance. Mick Davern was delighted and had a few pounds left over for the Company funds after paying for the revolver. Séumas Robinson supposed:

> This taste of the old care free life was only an appetiser to young Seán Hogan. After dancing all night in Ballagh he went off with a pretty girl from Glenough to another dance in Meagher's of Enfield. I had left the dance in Ballagh early in the night, Seán Treacy and Breen followed sometime after. We knew that Hogan was with the O'Keeffe girl at the dance in Ballagh, and we expected he'd be late. Seán Treacy had warned Mick Davern to keep an eye on Hogan and make sure that he'd come straight to O'Keeffe's after the dance. Mick has told the story of how artfully the dodger dodged him.

Next morning Robinson, Treacy and Breen were wakened by Paddy Kinane, a local Volunteer, who burst into the room and almost indignantly asked "'Do you fellows not know that one of your fellows is arrested.'" It was no surprise for them to hear about an arrest but the big question was; who?

Excitedly, according to Robinson, 'Paddy pointed at us and repeated "One of your chaps." "Is it young Hogan," asked Dan. The three of us got up and dressed quickly in silence. The first thing that came to my mind was one of Seán Hogan's dicta: "Ireland will never be free until she can produce a Robert Emmet who doesn't give a damn about women." He evidently didn't think Éire was capable of producing any such thing.'

Robinson stipulated that there was, from the beginning, a gentleman's understanding among 'The Big Four' that they would all stand or fall together. 'There was never a doubt in our minds that we'd rescue Hogan or pass out for good; but we wanted to do it to the best advantage that is, with a clean getaway. Treacy was even jocose about the sensation the rescue would cause.' From information received, they knew Hogan was brought to Thurles.

In the first instance, Hogan's comrades thought about cycling or getting a motor car and rushing the RIC barracks. Robinson thought that this would have been a viable option if they were certain that the police didn't know who the prisoner was and their guard would be down. Paddy Kinane was able to tell them that Hogan had not been identified yet, but that policemen were on their way from Tipperary Town to identify him. By the time they would be able to get into Thurles the identity of the prisoner would be ascertained, and the RIC would be well prepared for any rescue attempts. Stationed in Thurles was District Inspector Hunt, who was known for his vigour in pursuit of Republicans. It was always speculated that Hogan was mistreated while in custody here. Hunt would later be shot dead by the IRA in what probably was the first deliberate targeting of a specified RIC member due to his robust investigation into the subsequent rescue of Hogan.

Thurles has good rail connections so it was possible that Hogan could be taken to Dublin or Cork and perhaps even transported locally to Tipperary Town. Robinson believed that, 'If Hogan were taken to Dublin, I knew I could organise between the

Kimmage Garrison and the Dublin Brigade (men well known to me) sufficient numbers of determined men to storm the court. If he were brought to Tipperary Town it would be a relatively simple matter, but if to Cork that was terra incognita to us then - well, he must not be allowed to reach it.' Cork was to be Hogan's destination.

The first place the train would stop at in the South Tipperary area would be Goold's Cross. Robinson sent a dispatch to Mick Davern ordering him to have as many men as he could arm mobilised under cover not more than half a mile from the station, and await further instruction. Davern carried out the command and was, by all accounts, a very disappointed man when no further orders arrived.

Remembering the events surrounding the rescue on 13 May 1919, Robinson recollected:

Seán Treacy, who was Vice Commandant and therefore Director of Organisation (than whom there was none better) suggested that it would be better not to attempt the rescue before Limerick Junction to see if Hogan would be brought to Tipperary Town where there were more arms, and more Volunteers could be mobilised more easily and quicker. I agreed sorrowfully but not reluctantly. I would have liked my old Battalion and Company to have had the honour of assisting us. It was then decided to attack the train at Emly or Knocklong. Treacy was deputed to mobilise the Galbally Volunteers whom he knew to be first class men. His dispatches were many and quick. The Thurles Volunteers were asked to display no curiosity or excitement either at the barracks or the railway station. One man was to be casually knocking about in the station and to board it if Hogan were on it. Micksy O'Connell was the man.

A system of coded telegrams was devised to relay any additional information. Robinson, Treacy and Breen went to the house of a sympathiser about a mile from Knocklong Station. Every train from early morning was watched.

Ned O'Brien, a Volunteer from Galbally, picks up the story:

Mounted on bicycles, either our own or borrowed for the occasion, we started for Knocklong, and on the way, I think, both John Joe [O'Brien's brother] and Sean Lynch contacted Ned Foley of Duntreleague who also came along, and was subsequently executed in Mountjoy for his part in the fight. We all arrived at Maloney's in Lackelly sometime about three - thirty in the afternoon, where we met Seán Treacy, Dan Breen and Séumas Robinson. After a consultation there it was decided that we should divide the party, and that Seán Lynch, Jim Scanlon, my brother John Joe and Ned Foley would proceed to Emly station, and, as quietly as possible, board the train there with a view to discovering in what compartment the prisoner and his escort were travelling. As transpired subsequently, these men did their work very effectively. They boarded the train without having to buy the tickets at the station, they bought them from the guard as the train was about to start, and they got in without being seen by any of the enemy forces who happened to be on the train.

In the meantime, Seán Treacy, Dan Breen, Séumas Robinson and O'Brien proceeded on bicycles by road from Maloney's, via Knockarron and on to a place known locally as the 'Cross of the Tree.' Here, they dismounted on a quiet part of the road to consider the situation. Someone in the group suggested that four of them cycling together directly to Knocklong might look a bit suspicious if they happened to be observed, so it was decided to split up.

At the 'Cross of the Tree,' Seán Treacy and O'Brien cycled to the left up by the Catholic Church, around by the cemetery and down into the railway station. Séumas Robinson and Dan Breen proceeded by the main road straight to Knocklong. At a quiet bend in the road, the four reunited.

Treacy then asked O'Brien to proceed down to the coal store in Knocklong and ask if the manager had any telegrams for him. On arrival at the coal store, O'Brien told the manager, Tom Shanahan, who he was and asked if had he any message for Seán Treacy. O'Brien then recalled:

> He immediately became all attentive, took out his pocket-book and gave me a telegram. When I got the message, I jumped on my bicycle and cycled over the hill again to the other side of the railway to where I had left the others, and around the bend to where the three boys were waiting in the shadows for me. Seán opened the telegram immediately, and, as far as I remember, the wording of the telegram was, "Greyhound still in Thurles." I did not know what code was arranged, but the wording of it seemed to me to indicate that the operation was off for that evening anyway, and Seán immediately confirmed that impression.

After a short discussion on the matter, it was agreed that Dan Breen and Séumas Robinson should return to the road. They did not want to be seen milling around the station together. Treacy and O'Brien would wait for the arrival of the four Volunteers who had gone to Emly station and who were to come by train to Knocklong.

Around this time every evening a number of trains would converge at Knocklong. Sometimes there might be a few minutes interval, one pulling out before the other got in. That particular evening, Treacy and O'Brien were in the waiting room, opposite the station house buildings on the other platform, when the train to Dublin from Cork was signalled. This was about 7pm, just as dusk was descending. Amongst the passengers were some RIC men from Galbally station who had been conveying some prisoners to Cork jail that morning. The police were returning and they alighted at Knocklong station, which was unusual as they always went straight to Galbally. They proceeded on foot down the road.

In the meantime, the Dublin train pulled out of the station. As it did so, Treacy and O'Brien could see, a few hundred yards back along the line, the Cork-bound train approaching. Was Hogan on the train? O'Brien remembered thinking, in the moments beforehand that Hogan was not on board:

> My feelings at the time were, that it was only a matter of form to wait until the train had pulled in to collect our comrades. Whatever else was to happen afterwards I did not know. The train stopped at the station, and on looking at the carriages I saw at once the four Galbally lads at the window of a carriage. I moved quickly towards where they were, and the first one I spoke to, as he happened to be nearest to me at the time, was my brother. I knew by his attitude that the situation was not as I had thought it was, and that something very exceptional was on his mind. Then he whispered quickly to me, "They are in the next carriage." I moved rapidly towards where Seán Treacy was, and said to him, "Here they are in the next carriage." He did not hesitate for a moment, but gave the order to "Come on."

O'Brien followed Treacy. Drawing their guns, they mounted the train. The Galbally Volunteers immediately followed. The corridor was on the left-hand side of the train. They moved swiftly down along the corridor to where, as had been indicated, Hogan and his guard were located.

Seán Treacy slid the compartment door open. It glided along a track and, simultaneously, they entered and ordered "hands up" while they covered the armed police with their guns. For a moment O'Brien thought it was going to be a bloodless victory. Then he noticed that one of the RIC men, the only one wearing a revolver, had it drawn and was pointing it at Hogan. O'Brien instinctively opened fire and shot the RIC man dead.

What happened next was rather confused in the memory survivors. O'Brien recalled a frantic scene:

> Seán Treacy was in handgrips with a powerful Sergeant, and I remember being on the floor for a period. I remember Seán Lynch, Jim Scanlon and Foley coming into the compartment. One of the R.I.C. men at this stage jumped on the seat, and, as I was just rising to my feet at this time, I got the idea he was going to jump on me. This man, whose name I learned afterwards was Ring, sprang from the carriage seat and jumped head foremost right through the window, landing on the platform apparently unhurt.

The struggle then was hand to hand. O'Brien's gun was knocked out of his hand after he had fired a couple of shots, and it was picked up by Jim Scanlon and handed back to him later that night.

Treacy and the RIC Sergeant called Wallace were in a deadly encounter, swaying to and fro in their efforts to overcome each other. In the midst of all the pandemonium Seán Hogan was assisted out of the carriage. He was still handcuffed and had to fight his way out from the escort, striking at them with his manacled hands clenched together.

The carriage was crammed. Jim Scanlon and Seán Lynch wrestled the rifle from Constable O'Reilly. He was then hit over the head with the rifle butt, knocking him, seemingly, unconscious. However, he was only temporarily incapacitated and would soon make an unwelcome intervention.

While the fight in the carriage was in progress, Dan Breen and Séumas Robinson, who had gone back to the road, hastened back towards the station when they heard the sound of gunfire. Word was meant to have been sent to Robinson and Breen, who were concealed outside the station at the gate, if Hogan was on the train. Nevertheless, things did not transpire that way as Séumas Robinson later described:

> I think it well to mention that I guessed or surmised after the rescue, backed up by other incidents, that Seán [Treacy] wanted to carry out some things on his own. It had been arranged that the Galbally Volunteers would board the train at Emly if Hogan were on it. When the train arrived Treacy immediately led the crowd to the carriage where the R.I.C. and Hogan were. He did not send word as ordered to the two of us waiting at the gate. The first notice we got was the report of firing. Dan Breen seemed to have guessed at once that Hogan was on the train, he made a burst thro' the gate. I followed with vengeance in my heart. I thought that as Treacy hadn't sent word that some fool Volunteer had seen a soldier armed and couldn't resist the temptation to seize it. That would have put the 'caip bháis' [death sentence] on our hopes of a surprise attack when the train did arrive. In the heat of that awful moment I was determined to shoot off-hand whoever was guilty. As I got to the platform, I noticed Micksy O'Connell with the newspaper in his hand and realised that Hogan was on the train. Dan Breen hadn't reached the carriage where the fight had already taken place when Constable O'Reilly started to fire at the already retreating Volunteers. Dan was such a big target that O'Reilly didn't miss him. This Constable

picked off at least two others – O'Brien and Scanlon. We were soon all outside the gate attending to Breen who got a severe bullet wound below the collarbone. I asked anxiously what on earth had happened when someone said "Where is Hogan?" I dashed into the station and found Hogan smiling with his handcuffs on trying to scale a wall! I led him out.

It was thought that Constable O'Reilly was knocked unconscious by Lynch and Scanlon. He recovered and crawled out along the floor of the carriage on to the platform, and opened fire with his rifle on those who were still within the carriage. This coincided with Robinson and Breen entering the station. O'Reilly and Dan Breen opened fire on each other. O'Reilly's bullet hit Breen in the right shoulder and knocked the gun out of his hand. Breen picked up the gun with his good arm, and along with Robinson, fired and forced O'Reilly to retreat.

Despite all the gunfire, Treacy was still grappling with Wallace. O'Brien recollected that at one point during the struggle, his brother John Joe, who was armed with a small .32 automatic, fired point-blank at the Sergeant. The gun misfired, whereupon he pistol whipped the policeman, which opened a large wound on his forehead that bled profusely. The end of this epic fight was within sight. O'Brien recalled:

Seán Treacy and the Sergeant were still struggling in the narrow corridor. The Sergeant was a much heavier man and had the advantage in the confined space, while Seán's main effort was to prevent him from using his gun. They were struggling fiercely when I came to Seán's assistance by putting my arms around the Sergeant from behind and pulling him backwards until he reached the ground. At this time the carriage was practically empty. The prisoner and the other boys had gone. Apparently, the Sergeant had been dangerously wounded, and at this stage he collapsed. I went out the left-hand side, and I think Seán went out by the right. Seán had received a severe wound through the throat, it was near the windpipe, I believe, I was told afterwards.

As Ned O'Brien came from the station, he found his brother John Joe, Seán Lynch, Jim Scanlon and Ned Foley coming from a butcher's shop with Seán Hogan, with the handcuffs in his hands. One of the Volunteers had Constable O'Reilly's rifle. The handcuffs had been broken on the butcher's block by using a meat cleaver.

Séumas Robinson wanted to ensure that everyone was accounted for. Chaos reigned, passengers fled in all directions, people where sheltering everywhere from the gunfire. A number of Volunteers were wounded and bleeding heavily, and there was no sign of Treacy. Robinson asked:

"But where is Seán Treacy?" I wanted to know. No one knew. "He was in the carriage with us" I was told. As Seán didn't turn up I became very anxious and got the whole crowd to disperse after Hogan's handcuffs were removed. Breen was weak with loss of blood and they hastened him away with Hogan. There was general delight among them all because of the success of the rescue. It didn't occur to any of them that anything could have happened to Treacy. "He must have got out the other side of the train."

Robinson thought that was plausible, but Seán Treacy would have made his way to where the rest of them were. There was no sign of him. Robinson moved along the station outside the hedge to just beyond the engine where there was another gate. He stood up on the gate and scanned the fields and hedgerows. Then he saw two civilians searching the hedge on the other side of the train. They looked like two British officers in civvies; it appeared they were armed. With his trench coat, leggings and hand in pocket caressing his revolver, Robinson glared in their direction to let them know they were being watched. After a few moments one of them glanced round and saw Robinson, and at the same time spoke to his companion, who immediately straightened up and dusted his trousers. The men sauntered back towards the train.

The fact that these two had been searching the hedge was a good indication someone had gone that way. Robinson made his way by bicycle to Maloney's, the only house or people that he knew in the whole district. It was nerve-racking for him to be alone in unfamiliar territory, and he imagined that the wires must have been hot with calls for police and military reinforcements. He was keen to locate Treacy and make good his escape:

I had about a mile to go before I could get off the main road and under cover. To add to my discomfort the chain of the bike kept coming off. When I reached Maloney's I found them all hilariously delighted. "J.J. is rescued, J.J. is rescued!" ("J.J." stood for John Joe Hogan as Seán was also known). When I spoke of my anxiety about Seán Treacy they all laughed it off: "Yerra, nothing could happen to Seán!"

Sometime before this, during their life on-the-run, Robinson, Treacy, Breen and Hogan had been in this area. Noticing a peculiar formation in a mountain, Séumas Robinson remarked that particular shape must be noticeable for miles around. Seán Treacy replied in the affirmative and pointed out there is a great family living at the foot of it called Foley. They agreed that if ever they got separated in this area, for any reason, they would rendezvous at Foley's.

We all agreed, not thinking that the occasion would arise so soon. On our second visit to Maloney's we had been so taken up with the need to rescue Hogan that we never thought of fixing a rendezvous in case of necessity. In any case we couldn't imagine the four of us being separated after the coming rescue.

At Maloney's house, Robinson was informed that Hogan and Breen were already taken to Foley's. He had to wait till nightfall before anyone could risk going that direction. When he arrived, he found that Seán Treacy had in fact made his way there too. Seán had been shot through the neck by Wallace, with the bullet passing between the windpipe and the jugular vein. He had a very lucky escape. A doctor was summoned at once.

According to Robinson, the doctor patched up Breen and started on Seán Treacy, probing to find the passage of the bullet:

When the probing instrument came out at last at the other side of the wound the Doctor stepped back with arms akimbo, head to one side admiring his handiwork like a thrush eyeing a worm. He was a clever doctor and, like most really clever people, was quite a simple soul. While still holding his admiring posture, he explained the near miraculous passage of the bullet. The Doctor turned up early next morning and went thro' the same routine. He ordered Breen immediate rest; he was not to be removed... The Doctor, was insistent that Dan Breen should not be removed; but there was no alternative as the Foley's were too well known to risk staying any longer there. By this time, I was so fatigued from want of three nights' sleep without sitting down except to snatch a meal, that I scarcely remember our leaving Foley's. Dan was in great pain. The pony and trap we took to the road in, was so very jolty on the hilly roads that Dan had to be held from falling forward or backward. We reached West limerick and were brought to a house on a hilly place where we had a short rest. Seán

Treacy's wound did not dampen his spirits, he was as full of energy as ever and I don't think he lost a moment's sleep.

Seán Treacy made all the arrangements with the local Volunteers to procure transport to take them to the Shannon. They were going to go to County Clare. There were not many private motor cars in those days, and fewer still whose owners could be trusted. Military lorries and official motor cars were plentiful and constantly on the road since Hogan's rescue.

When scouts reported that a motor car had turned off the main road and was coming towards the house in which they were staying, Robinson became alarmed. Treacy and Breen were soon ready to take to the road to fight. Séumas Robinson begged the two of them to move off at once. Due to their injuries, progress would have to be slow. Robinson and Hogan would fight a delaying action, but neither Treacy nor Breen would move, they were prepared to fight or die.

Treacy saw that Breen's revolver was in working order and had his own ready for action. Despite everything that had transpired, courage was definitely not lacking in 'The Big Four.' Hogan and Robinson went outside armed with Mills Bombs, carbines and revolvers, to meet whatever fate had sent them. The scouts had moved down and discovered, just in time, that the occupants of the car were friends.

Robinson was quick to point out that Seán Hogan

> ...had just come through the nerve-racking experience of his capture and 'bloody' release without a quiver. He was only 18 years of age and he stood beside me as cool as the proverbial cucumber. When the men in the car came up to him to shake hands, he smilingly warned them that he thought it would be better to wait till he could get the pin back in the bomb!

In a couple of days, they reached Michael Brennan's Brigade area in County Clare, where they were comfortable for some weeks while Seán Treacy and Dan Breen recuperated. Robinson recalled that while in Clare:

> I gave them some lessons in swimming and diving at which I was (relatively) an expert. Clean-living lads they got well in a remarkably short time. We had been so long away from Dublin that we thought it well to go there to see how things were developing at Headquarters and be on the prowl for arms, our chronic need!

The RIC was in no doubt that the Soloheadbeg men were responsible for the rescue. They were also aware of local involvement, and many raids and arrests were carried out. Two men, Paddy Maher and Ned Foley, were executed for involvement, although only one of them was actually involved. Both these men were buried in the grounds of Mountjoy and received Irish State funerals in October 2001 as part of the ceremony for 'The Forgotten Ten.' Knocklong had further projected 'The Big Four' into local folklore and moved the country a step closer to war. Songs and stories circulated in the locality celebrating the daring rescue:

> *The news has spread through Ireland*
> *and spread from shore to shore*
> *Of such a deed, no living man has ever heard before*
> *From out a guarded carriage mid a panic-stricken throng*
> *Seán Hogan, he was rescued at the station of Knocklong*

In Dublin 'The Big Four,' having the necessary skill and experience as well as willingness to take action, were to be utilised in a new development – a clandestine war fought in the shadows of the capital with the aim of eliminating Britain's eyes and ears. A campaign directed against the political detectives of 'G' Division was about to commence.

CHAPTER SIX

"THE SQUAD"

Active Service in Dublin: July to December 1919

By early 1919, Michael Collins as Director of Intelligence, in partnership with Chief of Staff Richard Mulcahy and Dublin Brigade OC Dick McKee, was surreptitiously preparing for an offensive against the British Intelligence apparatus. This triumvirate envisaged a dedicated unit attached to the Intelligence Department and drawn from the Dublin Brigade. Their purpose would be to attack British agents, especially the detectives of the Dublin Metropolitan Police 'G' Division, in order to provoke the military conflict that they regarded as inevitable and render British Intelligence powerless.

While in Dublin, 'The Big Four' were summoned to a meeting to form this GHQ active service unit. This was the embryonic stage of the unit that would later be famously known as 'The Squad.' Richard Mulcahy presided. He told the assembled men that they would be expected to do all sorts of 'jobs' but nothing that entailed more than the minimum of risk. He warned those present that if any of them were caught or killed they could be quite possibly disowned. Many of those at the meeting were perturbed at this latter suggestion, but no one said anything.

Mulcahy dismissed the assembly, telling the Volunteers that there was no compulsion on anyone to become a member of the unit. They were to go home and consider things for themselves and come back to another meeting fixed for some short time later.

According to Robinson, both Seán Treacy and Dan Breen were highly indignant at the idea of being told that they would:

> ...be repudiated if caught; Mulcahy's "possibly" was ignored! They discussed it with most of the other men after the meeting. I argued with them but I could not convince them that at that time it was the only sensible thing for G.H.Q. to do. The political and Army Headquarters were still comparatively free; nothing of a military-action nature was so far traceable to them.

Dáil Éireann, as of yet, had not been proclaimed an illegal assembly by the British. Robinson felt that this was good for the Movement as a whole and allowed the space for the Republican Government to be established.

> When the four of us arrived at the second meeting the only other man to turn up and sign on was Jim Slattery. Some weeks after another meeting was called and this time a large number of names were given in. What changed I don't know. At first, we were put on the track of 'G' men, then spies, then big game: Lord French.

This work was up close and personal, and not everyone was prepared to do it. A lot of groundwork had to be done in terms of shadowing the detectives, noting their routines, movements and picking the best locations to carry out the shootings with minimum risk. This work was also assisted by 'G' Division moles recruited by the IRA, such as Ned Broy, Jim Kavanagh, James McNamara and David Neligan.

Collins first familiarised himself with the British intelligence system. He infiltrated the postal and telegraph services which facilitated much of the communication in those days. Once a full picture had been built up, the IRA began eliminating its most prominent officers, agents and informers.

To decapitate 'G' Division, the Active Service Unit was formally established in mid-July 1919 and consisted of full-time Volunteers from McKee's Dublin Brigade. In these early stages, they were ably assisted by 'The Big Four' who had already demonstrated a willingness to use their weapons.

Located originally in a private house near Amiens Street, 'The Squad' eventually settled in Upper Abbey Street. Its secret headquarters was disguised as Moreland's cabinet-makers, upholsterers and builders. Here, the Squad posed as carpenters, though always carrying concealed weapons under their white aprons. On 30 July 1919, they shot their first 'G'-man, Patrick Smyth, a beginning had been made in this covert conflict.

After a number of shootings, Dublin Castle finally reacted by suppressing Dáil Éireann on 11 September 1919. That same day 'The Squad' executed 'G' Division's rising star, Detective Dan Hoey and soon afterwards Detective Sergeant Johnny Barton who was shot by Treacy. Both had been instrumental in screening prisoners after the Easter Rising. Subsequently, Collins went on-the-run, the Dáil Government Departments went underground, and the British Government suppressed Sinn Féin and the Irish Volunteers. The Viceroy, Lord French, declared: 'We are really at war now.' He was soon to find himself a target in this renewal of hostilities.

Séumas Robinson, as noted earlier, had prior history with Collins from his Kimmage days. Although not a member of the 'Garrison,' Collins was a frequent visitor due his connection with the IRB in general and Joseph Plunkett in particular. Collins was now a senior member of the IRB, an organisation that Robinson believed was a 'sinister cabal.' He was distrustful of the behind the scenes manipulation that was the preferred operating method of the IRB.

Robinson recorded that 'The first time I found Mick Collins to be a bit of an artful dodger was when he arranged the first 'phoney' attack on French.' Field Marshall John Denton Pinkstone French, 1st Earl of Ypres, was now the Viceroy of Ireland. He was the very person that represented the Crown and headed up British administration in Ireland. He was a target of major interest to the fledgling IRA campaign. A successful operation resulting in French's death would be a major coup.

Volunteer officers were in Dublin for a General Convention held in the autumn of 1919. The Convention was cancelled due to the deteriorating security situation, and before the delegates had time to go home, Collins rounded up officers from all parts of the country. He came personally to Mrs. Boland's of Clontarf to waken Breen and Robinson. Also staying in the house were Ned O'Brien and Jim Scanlon of Galbally, who both had assisted in the rescue of Hogan. Due to their role at Knocklong, they were being secreted out of Ireland to the USA. They would be personally escorted to their boat by the 'Big Four' to ensure they would not be arrested, something that both men never forgot.

Collins announced that they were to make an attempt on French's life. After supposedly receiving intelligence on the Viceroy's itinerary, it was reported that he was returning to Ireland from London and would arrive by boat. Travelling to Dublin Castle by car, the plan was to ambush him on the road. Various ambush positions along the way were manned by Volunteers, including officers who were to attend the Convention. Séumas Robinson wrote:

Mick gave Seán Treacy and me "they shall not pass" point to hold: the last corner French would pass before the Castle was reached. We were told that the convoy was to be attacked all the way from Dun Laoghaire; if French escaped these ambushes, we two were to see to it that he didn't get past us alive. We were to keep moving as if we were innocent civilians and yet we were to stay at our post! We were told that French was coming on the early mail boat to Dun Laoghaire, that he'd be driven by convoy to the Castle, and that it would not be later than 5a.m.

Treacy and Robinson passed the time walking up and down, not turning around till they were sure that no one was in sight to notice that they were loitering. Robinson began to realise that Seán always strode in front of him particularly as it drew near 5am.

I knew that Seán's sight was not very good so I kept close to him. At last Seán stopped and said with his usual grin: "Would you mind taking the driver I want to get the old josser." "All right Seán!" It was so close to zero hour that we didn't care who saw us we were out in the middle of the road to block the car.

As 5am struck, they heard the noise of a number of men walking around the corner talking loudly and laughing. They wheeled round to see who it was:

Round the corner from Dame Street came Mick Collins, Seán Ó Muirthile, Seán McGarry, Thomas McCurtain and others. "It's all right" shouted Mick "he isn't coming!" I was delighted to see Thomas McCurtain whom I hadn't seen since our Reading Gaol days. Thomas was delighted too, not at meeting me, but at having got a splendid revolver which he declared he wasn't going to part with!

Robinson learned much later that French, instead of being in Britain, was in fact at his Roscommon estate. There was no word at all of him coming to Dublin. Robinson felt that Collins was able to give the impression to the Volunteer officers from all over the country that he not only organised the attacks on spies that had begun in Dublin but also that he led them. 'Certainly, Mick organised this "attack" on French; he mobilised the men for it and he was out himself that morning. And that was the nearest I ever saw Mick Collins to a fight.'

Robinson apportioned much of the blame on Collins for the subsequent compromise that was the Treaty, which ultimately resulted in the Civil War. Again, he believed that it was the clandestine cloak and dagger approach of the IRB that was largely to blame. He noted:

> Towards the end of 1920 and the beginning of 1921, the British press had been changing its description of Collins from a "thug" and "murderer" to "a daredevil"; romanticising him with damnation that praised him in the sight of the Irish people. He was "seen" all over the country leading the columns from Dublin to West Cork where he had been "seen" riding on a white charger like King William at the Boyne. But it was Tom Barry who rode the horse because of a strained foot and King William rode a brown horse! This sort of journalism is not history but it is blatant propaganda. In the case of Mick Collins, it put him on a pedestal where he did not properly belong. It enhanced his undoubted influence beyond all bounds.

Robinson believed that the British press had received direction from their political masters; they were laying the ground for a compromise, and 'the anti-national press in Ireland simply quoted the English press without comment knowing the reports were false.' He could see the aim behind this personalised propaganda, and Robinson opined that when 'Collins treacherously signed The Articles for a Treaty in 1921 the anti-Republican press to a sheet became fulsome in their praise of Collins whom they would have handed over to the British if they could from 1916.'

Robinson stated publicly that Michael Collins never fired a shot during the years of struggle.

> No exception can be taken to me making that statement even now that Collins is dead because I challenged him (and any Deputy who cared to take up the challenge) to say if he ever fired even one shot at the British enemy during the Tan War or during Easter Week 1916. I made that challenge during the debates on the "Treaty."

However, he did concede that it would have been wrong for Collins to have exposed himself to danger during the Tan War. He was too important to the Army. 'And I should like to add no one ever heard him lay claim to the fantastic things attributed to him by the British press copied by the sycophantic Irish press without comment!'

After what Robinson described as the 'phoney' attack on French, there were other apparently serious attempts; all failed because of inaccurate information. Seán Hogan and Treacy were on these attempts. Robinson was back in Tipperary at this stage. However, he was in Dublin on Army business when he received word to be at the only attack that materialised at Ashtown.

On Friday 19 December 1919, a party drawn from the Active Service Unit, including Breen, Treacy, Hogan and Robinson, and numbering in all eleven Volunteers, proceeded to Ashtown to carry out the attack on the Viceroy. Their information was that Lord French would come by train to Ashtown at 11.40 am and that he would disembark the train there and travel by motorcade to the Viceregal Lodge in Phoenix Park.

The unit rode out the Cabra Road on bicycles, travelling two by two. Robinson remembered one of his comrades, Martin Savage, sang all the way, among his songs being "A soldier's life, is the life for me a soldier's death, so Ireland's free." The words of the song would be prophetic for Savage, who was apparently not part of the unit but was brought along by Seán Hogan; Savage's death would have a profound and lasting impact on Hogan.

The Volunteers arrived at Kelly's public house, Ashtown, which stands about 200 yards from Ashtown Station and about 100 yards from the Phoenix Park gate. Paddy Daly, who was in command of the party, gave out the instructions. A large body of men standing about the road would be sure to attract attention, so they were to go into the public house and mingle with customers and order some minerals, as if they were cyclists passing along the road. Shortly before the train was due to arrive, the Volunteers were to line the inside of the hedge on the right-hand side of the road for about thirty yards. Breen, Martin Savage and Tom Keogh were to barricade the road at the last moment by drawing a heavy cart, which stood close by, across the path of the coming cars. Breen and his two comrades had to, according to Robinson, do this with an air of innocence or stupidity 'because if they looked too business-like about it, they might rouse the suspicions of some of the people in the public house.'

The usual order in which the Viceregal party travelled was first a motor car carrying Lord French's armed escort, then the car in which Lord French sat and then another carrying the rest of his escort. Daly instructed them not to attack the first car but concentrate on the second.

The look-outs soon brought word that the train was signalled, and they all moved quietly and quickly to their allotted posts, all the time keeping out of sight. In order to prevent civilian casualties, men were placed at the cross roads to intercept passers-by.

Appreciating that Daly might not give much consideration at this eleventh hour to a proposal, Robinson made up his mind to withhold his own bomb in reserve until after the second car was dealt with. He felt with absolute certainty that if this precaution were not taken, the whole action might be marred by heavy casualties on their side.

The cars started from the station. The time had come for the road party to get into action, and they began slowly to pull the heavy cart across the road. While they were doing this, a DMP man suddenly appeared on the scene. Taking the barricaders for countrymen engaged in their work, he began to argue that they could not bring their cart that way. Feigning stupidity, the Volunteers tried to carry on with their duty.

The policeman kept explaining that the passage must be kept clear for "His Excellency" and he could not be persuaded to move on. At this point one of the ambush party settled the argument by throwing the only missile he had to hand at the policeman, namely, a bomb. He had not drawn the pin, so there was little danger of it exploding. This stunned the policeman, and almost at the same moment the Viceroy's car came into range. The road was not yet fully blocked by the cart.

The cars came close together as Robinson had hoped, and immediately the action began to unfold. All of the Volunteers, remembering their instructions, concentrated the attack on the second car, in which Lord French was thought to be travelling. Robinson recorded:

I, however, side-stepped orders and, waiting until the second car had been bombed out of action, hurled my bomb at the first car. What effect my bomb had I never heard with any certainty, but the car bounded away, crashing past the slight barricade. It was discovered afterwards that contrary to the usual custom, Lord French was seated in the first, instead of in the second car.

After hurling his bomb, Séumas Robinson rushed to where Dan Breen, Martin Savage and Tom Keogh were standing without any cover. He was anxious to make sure that there would be no enfilading of their position.

Now the third car, taking up the rear of the escort, came dashing along at a furious pace, bumping over and pushing aside obstacles on the road; the occupants were prepared to defend their charge with their lives. This was an open car and rifle fire directed from it took an immediate toll on the exposed Volunteers.

Robinson, in his account of the attack, vividly recalled:

In the back of the car stood a soldier, with his legs braced between the seats, his rifle held tight to his shoulder with the left hand, and his right hand working evenly, almost gracefully, on the bolt and trigger. This soldier was a sharpshooter. His first shot gave young Martin Savage his death wound; the second went through Breen's hat, grazing his head, and the third hit Breen in the leg, wounding him seriously. Breen, now out of action, limped painfully to cover in the public-house door, and a milk-cart, which, fortunately for me, came along the main road at this moment provided cover from which to continue the attack. I was sorry for that milkman but I had neither the time nor the inclination to consider his point of view.

After a concentration of fire from the Volunteers, the third car sped off. The second car had been badly damaged by their gunfire and bombs; it could not proceed any farther. As his comrades had fled, leaving him to the mercy of the Volunteers, the soldier who had been driving walked out with his hands up. The ambush was now over.

The attacking party came out on to the main road, and the soldier was disarmed. He was trembling and evidently expected to be shot, but he was treated with every courtesy by the Volunteers. He was obviously surprised and relieved when someone said: "'We are soldiers, too, and do not shoot unarmed prisoners.'"

Martin Savage had been killed, shot through the throat by the sharpshooter. His comrades debated whether they should take his body away with them, but it was decided that it would be impossible as they had only bicycles. They also had a wounded man to bring to safety. Treacy and Robinson stayed behind until Breen escaped the scene.

Breen was very weak from loss of blood, and his leg was useless, he could neither walk nor cycle by himself. He was helped on to his bicycle. Paddy Daly, riding his own bicycle and supporting Breen on the other, started on a difficult and perilous journey to reach the house of Mrs Twomey at Phibsborough, a few miles away.

Later Robinson and Treacy learned that Daly, Frank Thornton and the others brought their wounded comrade to the 'safe house' without incident. It would be more than a month before Breen was able to move without assistance.

As soon as the remainder of the unit were safely away, Treacy and Robinson jumped on their bicycles and started to ride at top speed from Ashtown, for they knew that the district would soon be swarming with British military and police searching for the IRA.

Robinson recollected that he:

> ...had hardly started when one of my pedals struck a stone, and came off; so, throwing my bicycle over a hedge, I got on the back of Treacy's machine. The bumping over stones made me press down on the rear mud guard, and Treacy soon found he could make no progress. Luckily for us a man came into view, wheeling a brand-new machine, and politely but firmly we told him that we would have to borrow it from him for a few hours. He was very indignant, and obviously did not believe me when I promised that it would be left for him at a certain place and at a certain hour that evening. I heard afterwards that this man was an R.I.C. pensioner. The bicycle was handed over to the Dublin A.S.U. to return it as best they could. With the unwilling help of that ex-policeman I was able to resume my journey into town with Seán Treacy and at last we arrived at Lynch's of Dolphin's Barn. Thinking at the time that Breen would be in Grantham Street, where his fiancée lived, we dared not go at once to 71 Heytesbury Street, our Dublin H.Q. for fear of drawing too much attention to the district.

After a quick wash and shave, Robinson and Treacy went out to enjoy the sensation caused by the attack on the Viceroy. Wild rumours were circulating through Dublin. Those who had been on the spot really believed that Lord French and his car had been blown to bits at Ashtown. Robinson, with a touch of humour, exclaimed 'I am sure that he [French] was as delighted as we were disappointed that this was not really the case, but, although the action was not successful in one way it certainly caused a panic in British Government circles.'

Dan Breen was subsequently taken to Malone's of Grantham Street. He was weak from loss of blood and only half conscious. A young priest was brought to hear his Confession, but someone had rushed in proclaiming aloud that Martin Savage's body had been refused admission to Phibsborough Chapel. Breen refused to go to Confession saying: "'If my dead body isn't fit to be taken into the Church then I'm not fit to be in it alive.'" The young priest was very nervous. The house was full of armed men. He was fumbling nervously with his stole. Arguments started for and against but when the Bishop's condemnation was referred to, it seemed to put a finish to all argument. Robinson felt that he needed to intervene:

> I hadn't said a word about this but I was very anxious about Dan not going to Confession. It occurred to me that this was one occasion where a Hail Mary was called for. I whispered it to myself, then, like an inspiration an idea occurred to me. I stepped up to the bed and said: "Look here, Dan, the way I look on this whole business is this: I won't mind so much going to hell for something I will have got a damned good kick out of but I'll be damned if I'll go to hell just to please the Bishops!" The apparent logic, coupled with the flavour of a fighting spirit behind it, worked. Dan thought for a moment then nodded towards the priest.

Breen would stay in Dublin to recuperate. He would remain in the city for most of the intervening period. Robinson and Treacy, meanwhile, were back and forth to Tipperary, refining their organisational infrastructure and pushing their men towards a war footing. Being absent from Tipperary, nevertheless, did have an impact on the area, and Robinson recalled:

> Sometime in 1919 Seán Treacy and Dan Breen had convinced me (I being a young and little-known City man)

that it would be better for us and the Movement as a whole if someone better known who would command the respect of the people in general were Brigade O/C., and Treacy suggested Frank Drohan as the most suitable man. Drohan was an I.R.B. man and in local politics. Thinking that Treacy knew his countrymen's psychology I agreed.

Treacy wrote to GHQ making the offer of the change, but Chief of Staff Richard Mulcahy, instead of a direct reply, sent Robinson a letter that was written to GHQ by Drohan in which he was complaining that 'The Big Four' were going around the countryside creating disturbance. Robinson instituted an inquiry into the whole working of the 5th Battalion. The result was that the whole staff was demoted except the Battalion Adjutant, Seán Quirke, who was the only officer able to clear himself beyond doubt of undermining the war effort. Robinson remained as Brigadier.

Following the capture of a dispatch-rider who had a document detailing the names and numbers of the Battalions then existing, Seán Treacy suggested a change in the Battalions. What was the First became the Fourth, the Second became the Third and the latest formed at Rathsallagh became the First. This latter Battalion soon became the Headquarters of the Brigade, located at Jerome Davin's home. The stage was now set for, what would prove to be the decisive year in the armed conflict between the IRA and the Crown Forces.

CHAPTER SEVEN

A GHOSTLY ARMY

Fighting for Irish Freedom: Tipperary 1920 – 21

While in Dublin both Séumas Robinson and Seán Treacy maintained regular contact with the Brigade organisation in Tipperary and often travelled back to their command area. Militant activity was increasing, and indeed both Robinson and Treacy were not afraid to produce their weapons and shoot their way through check points and searches when the need arose.

There is one story of Robinson being accosted by a policeman in Dublin for not having a light on his bicycle. Earlier in the day Robinson was staying with the O'Doherty family, and Mrs O'Doherty, who would later be the ghost writer of Breen's *My Fight for Irish Freedom*, had read his tea leaves. She warned him that he would be in a tight spot later that night and he would be fine if he did nothing. The hapless policeman proposed to Robinson that he would have to accompany him to the Bridewell to verify his identity. Séumas Robinson decided to shoot the policeman when they reached a dark spot under a railway bridge but he hesitated, remembering Mrs O'Doherty's warning. At that moment, the policeman changed his mind and sent Robinson on his way. Fortunately, for the policeman, fate had intervened and unbeknown to him he walked away with his life.

Mick Davern recalled that 'About the end of October 1919, a Brigade Convention was arranged to take place at Meldrum Hall,

Cashel.' He knew that Séumas Robinson, Seán Treacy and Seán Hogan were to attend. A friendly farmer, Con Dwyer, received a telegram from Dublin stating that "manures are being sent out today," a code by which they knew that their Brigade Officers were due to arrive that night.

Goold's Cross station was scouted before nightfall by a small number of Volunteers. Davern had a party of Volunteers close by. Some 20 minutes before the train was due to arrive, the local Section Commander reported four RIC had come from Clonoulty barracks and that they were on the station platform. Davern consulted with the Battalion Commandant, Tadhg Dwyer, and urged very strongly that they should shoot the police. However, Dwyer believed it should be their last resort and agreed if it was the only course left open to save their Brigade Officers from an unpleasant surprise, and possibly death, then they would shoot the RIC men.

Michael Sheehan, acting Brigade Quartermaster, gave definite instructions to the Volunteers that the police were not to be shot. He said that if the four were shot they could not hold the Convention and Martial Law would be re-established. Davern argued that if any of their officers were shot or arrested, they definitely could not hold any Convention. He articulated the fact that the element of surprise was with the RIC and that Robinson, Treacy and Hogan coming off the train would have to walk up the steps into their arms. Therefore, they had to do something.

Davern ordered some of his own men to take off their boots so that they could get within range of the RIC without being heard. Before a final decision was reached, the train was heard coming into the station. Davern and Dwyer had no other option but to warn their comrades on the train. They ran about 200 or 250 yards and jumped right into the station, shouted at Robinson, Treacy and Hogan to follow them. They immediately ran to the front of the train, pursued by the RIC who commenced firing. Volunteers fired from their position at the top of the Bridge at the RIC who seemed to ease their fire, with the result that the three men for whom the British Government was offering thousands of pounds reward escaped untouched.

The RIC retired into the stationmaster's house for the rest of the night. In the course of the fight, Seán Hogan lost a portmanteau containing ammunition and documents. It was too dark to see it, and time was of the essence so they had to move on. Fortunately, the bag was found by the signalman going off duty in the morning, and he hid it in a heap of coal. The following day, the father of a local Volunteer visited the store for coal, and the signalman handed over the bag.

Robinson, Treacy and Hogan went to Glenough, then on to Doon where a motor car, belonging to the local bank manager, was commandeered. They were driven back to Dublin in order to throw the RIC off their scent. Shortly afterwards, the Brigade Convention was held in Meldrum Hall, and all the senior officers of the Brigade were assembled with exception of 'The Big Four.' Robinson and Treacy had left instructions for the Brigade Officers to discuss plans for organisation and for developing the fight in the locality. Leadership was very much required to provide a strong focus and give direction at this key stage, so both Robinson and Treacy would soon return. Their presence would have a visible impact in the coming months.

The RIC, believing that Robinson, Treacy and Hogan were back in the area, began a number of intensive searches. A number of local officers were arrested, including Davern. He was brought to Clonoulty Barracks:

I was going in the door of the barracks; I was kicked by Sergeant Maloney. Constable Twomey struck a vicious swiping blow at my head with his rifle and, had I not ducked, the murderous blow would certainly have killed me. Before Twomey had recovered I struck him a few times, only to receive blows and kicks from about a dozen R.I.C. who had come into the day room. They continued to kick and beat me while on the floor with shouts of "Where is Robinson and Treacy for you now?" Murtagh, a young Constable, shouted: "You are only a pack of cowards to beat a young fellow like that; he's only a kid." The rest of them shouted: "He's a bloody murderer and we always knew it." This young Constable Murtagh was shot dead some three weeks afterwards on Christmas morning 1919 by Constable Twomey. But at the subsequent inquiry, the verdict was "accidental death." During that night I had heard Twomey saying that Murtagh should join the I.R.A., and Murtagh replied: "Maybe I might."

Tipperary was, once again, like a powder keg ready to explode. The RIC were still frustrated that they had not captured 'The Big Four' and the Volunteers became more brazen in hold-ups and arms raids. They were more willing to use their weapons. More and more men had to 'go on-the-run.'

Robinson, on returning to the locality, used the opportunity of having more full-time activists. He noted that:

> As these men increased in numbers, they were banded together into what we called "Active Service Groups." When I reported this to G.H.Q. they adopted the idea but gave them the better name of "Active Service Units." Columns were the next step suggested by G.H.Q.

The 'Ghostly Army' envisaged earlier by Robinson began to take shape. He would take into consideration the prevailing circumstances in the Brigade area and adopt his tactics and strategy accordingly:

I was not enamoured of the idea of large Columns. To me they seemed to approximate too closely to a small standing Army which was objectionable from several points of view. (1) They were a permanent large body and therefore too easily located and the loss of a Column would have meant almost completely disarming the Brigade. They required every available rifle. (2) They required too many Volunteers as extra guards and dispatch carriers, most of whom were needed at home to keep the home-fires burning and the pot boiling for us as well as for themselves. Big Columns used to eat, almost out of house and home, a whole townland; and, compared to the usefulness-beyond the nuisance 'value' to the enemy-of their military actions during long periods, their upkeep was rather costly. (3) There was the danger of the slow-moving British awakening-up to the one counter action that I feared: organising ten Columns to our one. It was putting the idea into their heads. In fact, it was in our Brigade area that they [the British Military] first experimented with a large Flying Column.

To illustrate his point further, Robinson gave the example of the Davin family. Their household was at the disposal of the IRA. Besides local Volunteers and Brigade staff-officers, there were many callers from GHQ, the eight Battalions that made up the Third Tipperary Brigade and dispatch-riders that the Davins were approaching financial difficulties. A large number of farmers and sympathisers found themselves in a similar position.

These people housed, fed and clothed the Volunteers. Whole Columns would on occasions be billeted for two to three days at a time. These good people were too proud to drop even a hint of their monetary distress. It was only by an accident that Robinson discovered this state of affairs, so he decided to spread the burden a little more evenly by asking GHQ to allow him to issue a levy-appeal to the people. He felt that this was a people's struggle and that the people of South Tipperary would not be found wanting and would support them. The levy was introduced successfully in the area, was adopted by GHQ and was subsequently incorporated into standing orders to be implemented nationally.

Militant activities took place with a more regular frequency, shootings, ambushes and concentrated attacks, such as those on troop trains, destruction of British infrastructure and apparatus throughout the county. The year 1920 would see an escalation of the war. Smaller garrisons and RIC barracks were evacuated, and they amassed their forces in stronger positions. Robinson pointed out:

> ...about the end of March, 1920, the R.I.C. left the barracks at Lisronagh very near our Brigade Headquarters. I immediately wrote to G.H.Q. pointing out the necessity for its destruction and suggesting that this applied to all other vacated R.I.C. barracks all over the country, and that if a General Order were issued for a definite date the element of surprise would be ours. I feared that if we burned Lisronagh Barracks first the British authorities might awaken to the advisability of reoccupying these [smaller] barracks, strengthening them and manning them better. G.H.Q. issued an order to destroy all vacated R.I.C. barracks in the country.

Word seems to have been sent to the RIC in Clonmel because Lisronagh was reoccupied secretly. The RIC were lying in ambush for the Volunteers who were under orders to destroy the barracks. The police opened fire, and the demolition unit were taken completely by surprise. They had great difficulty in fighting their way out, but did so without any serious casualties.

The various barracks positioned throughout the Brigade area were now a firm target, whether occupied or not. Robinson stated:

When anything big was on, I tried to be there, such as in the attacks on barracks or troop trains. I was on the roof at the destruction of Hollyford barracks with Ernie O'Malley, and on the roof at the capture of Drangan barracks with Seán Treacy. Both these fights lasted about six hours.

As a GHQ organiser, O'Malley travelled around the country to support IRA commands with training, organisation and attacks. He had gained valuable experience of attacks on barracks, most notably at Ballytrain, County Monaghan, in February 1920.

O'Malley relished being in Tipperary with officers who could think and act for themselves, who were prepared to fight, and, perhaps more importantly for him, were good shots and acted without fear. They were constantly on alert and were ready to engage the enemy as they travelled around the command area. O'Malley wrote:

> During the day we eased the springs of our automatic magazines in turn by withdrawing cartridges. Automatics would have the hammer cocked with the safety catches on; rifles, if we carried them, had a bullet in the breech. If we met trouble it would mean a sudden quick action in which every second counted. At night, with revolvers or automatics in hand we moved in file along lanes and roads, walking quietly; the collars of coats buttoned up to cover the whites of our throats.

There was a great sense of camaraderie between them. Discussions were held about past campaigns, they spoke of literature, of Irish language and all aspects of Gaelic culture. In a scene that would be powerfully portrayed in the film 'The Wind that Shakes the Barley,' Ernie O'Malley recalled that Séumas Robinson was looking a marching song for the Brigade. 'He would try out the notes. Seán's cracked spindle of voice would join and I would help the discord.'

164

'Sé do bheatha, a bhean ba léanmhar
do bé ár gcreach tú bheith i ngéibhinn
do dhúiche bhreá i seilbh meirleach
's tú díolta leis na Gallaibh.

Óró, sé do bheatha bhaile
óró, sé do bheatha bhaile
óró, sé do bheatha bhaile
anois ar theacht an tsamhraidh.

They talked tactics, held training for Volunteers and IRA Officers but, more importantly, they wanted to put this all into action. Their attention turned to the small RIC Barracks that were dotted around the command. They embarked upon a series of attacks with the express aim of destroying these garrisons.

These attacks became the stuff of legend and are eloquently recorded by Ernie O'Malley in his seminal work *On Another Man's Wound*. The attack on Hollyford RIC barracks took place on the night of 12 May 1920. Ernie O'Malley, Séumas Robinson, Seán Treacy and Seán Hogan had spent the previous few days and nights with Tadgh Dwyer in his Battalion area, and he recalled with certainty that it was while they were staying at O'Keeffe's of Glenough that it was decided to attack Hollyford. Plans to carry it out were quickly devised.

The barracks was a long, two-storied building, standing aloof from any of the other houses in the village. It was permanently garrisoned by about 12 RIC men and its windows were steel shuttered and loop holed. There was no house near enough to it which the IRA could possibly occupy as a key point of attack and from which the roof of the barracks could be set on fire.

After a long discussion, it was decided to use ladders to gain access to the roof. Dwyer was appointed to make arrangements for the procurment of the ladders and for hoisting them against the barrack wall. The walls were about 30 feet high. No ladders long enough for the job could be sourced locally, so it was arranged with a local tradesman to splice a number of ladders together to make two of sufficient height.

Meanwhile, arrangements were made to obstruct the roads leading to Hollyford and for the manning of these road blocks. Practically all members of the Battalion who were not actually assigned a position in Hollyford were engaged in this work. They also received assistance from other adjoining areas. Brian Shanahan, Commandant of the 4th Battalion and some of his men held a post on the road between Tipperary Town and Hollyford, while other men from the Brigade held the road to Thurles.

At Phil Shanahan's family farmhouse, about a mile from Hollyford, the final arrangements were made on the day of the attack. 'Mud Bombs' were made by moulding sticky wet clay around a stick of gelignite; these were designed to adhere to walls or slates. The men assigned to the ladders rehearsed their drill. This was a necessary manoeuvre, as they needed to be able to do it quickly and noiselessly when it came to placing it against the barrack wall. It was a tricky and delicate job. That night a supply of paraffin oil and inflammable materials were deposited in the local creamery, located about 80 yards from the barracks. Men were detailed to draw the oil in buckets from the creamery as required.

The attack started about midnight. Riflemen had assumed positions on all four sides of the barracks. In bare feet, Volunteers approached the barrack with the ladder and successfully raised it into position at the first attempt. While it was held in place, Séumas Robinson and Ernie O'Malley, carrying the equipment they required on their backs, climbed the ladder and got on to the roof. O'Malley vividly describes the scene:

Séumas and I had two revolvers each, grenades, bursting charges, supplies of fuse, detonators and hammers to smash slates. On our backs a tin of petrol was tied, sods of turf that had been soaked in oil were slung around our necks by cords. The oil sopped into our clothes. The men with the ladders took off their boots; they tied them around their necks...The ladders were placed in position; Séumas' was to one side, mine against the chimney. I intended to sit on it to fire through the roof. I just hoped the Peelers would not use their rifles through the flue. Buckets of paraffin and petrol were placed on the ground near the ladders.

Local Volunteer William Hanley, who was assigned to the ladder unit, recalled in detail the events of that night:

Ernie O'Malley, G.H.Q. staff, Seán Treacy and Séumas Robinson from the South Tipperary Brigade were in charge, and there were also men present from the Mid Tipperary Brigade. Tom Carey and I were put into a section of about twelve men whose job it was to place two ladders at the gable corner of the barracks nearest to the Foilmacduff or Shanahan's Road. Great stress was placed in the instructions which were given to us regarding the importance of putting these ladders into position as silently as possible. The least move might alert the police, who had loopholes cut in the gable from which grenades could be dropped that would blow us all to pieces. Between 11 and 12 o'clock that night our section moved off from Shanahan's with the two ladders, the smaller men being in front and the taller men behind to facilitate the raising of the ladders against the barrack walls. In front of the barracks a number of roads met, I think five, all told, including the laneway up to Shanahan's house. There was no wall between the barracks and the crossroads and this facilitated our approach to the building. Under O'Malley's direction the ladders were quickly put into position, one in front, about two feet from the gable corner, and the other against the gable, also about two feet from the same corner.

These attacks were an important development in the escalation of the conflict in the locality. The officers were leading from the front, placing themselves in a perilous position. Valuable experience would be gained by everyone involved in the attack. Hanley continued with his account:

O'Malley and Robinson scaled the ladders… On getting to the roof, these two men broke a hole in the slates with hammers and then pumped the petrol through the hole. In a short period, the flames were to be seen rising from the barracks, but this did not seem to have any great effect on the police garrison. After having placed the ladders in position and seeing O'Malley and Robinson safely on the roof, myself and the men who carried the ladders went back to the Foilmacduff Road to await developments. There were also two sections armed with rifles, one behind a low wall near the creamery on the far side of the road opposite the front of the barracks, and the section in the fields at the rear of the barracks behind a fence roughly a hundred yards from that building. From memory I would estimate the strength of each section at seven or eight men. As soon as O'Malley and Robinson had got on the roof these riflemen opened fire on the front and rear of the barracks, and kept up this fire until the order to retreat was given about six o'clock next morning. The police spared no ammunition either and from the outset to the finish replied vigorously with rifle fire. For the want of having nothing else to do, I went to join the riflemen at the rear of the barracks and

168

remained with them until we retired. Seán Treacy, who appeared to have charge of both sections of the riflemen, kept moving from one to the other. Of course, all hopes of taking the building were based on burning it and thus force the garrison to come out and surrender.

As Robinson and O'Malley worked on the roof, the men on the ground had opened a slow steady fire, aiming at the windows and door of the barracks. The RIC replied with rifle fire and rifle grenades. At intervals, they also fired Verey lights. These flares lit up the sky either in an attempt to summons help or to aid the identification of targets.

As alluded to by Hanley, the success of the attack depended mainly on the efforts of O'Malley and Robinson to ignite the barracks and thus compel the garrison to surrender. Those observing from the ground appreciated that their task on the roof was a difficult and unenviable one. To a certain extent, things did go according to plan; after a time, they succeeded in breaking through the slates and getting the roof timbers and ceilings burning. It was literally heating up for the two IRA officers. O'Malley continued his narrative:

> Séamus and I looked at each other. The hair was burnt off his head, his face was black, red and blistered, he had no eyebrows. My face felt strange. My eyelashes and eyebrows had gone; there were raised ridges on my face and head and on the back of my neck; my hands stung most of all. Our clothes were burnt in patches, and soaked with oil and petrol. We laughed at each other whilst we wrung our hands in pain.

The police had taken refuge in a small room which was separated by a thick dividing wall from the main portion of the barracks, described as a lean-to building. All efforts to set this portion of the barracks on fire and put the RIC garrison in an untenable position failed. The garrison held out, and by 7am things had reached a stalemate. The RIC could not be dislodged, and with the coming of daylight and the hope of the early arrival of reinforcements the garrison were not likely to surrender.

According to Hanley he thought that by 5am it looked as if the attack was going to succeed. Practically all of the barracks was in flames and by then there was no firing coming from the rear, and at the front only from a stout stone porch.

It was this porch which saved the situation for the enemy. It did not take fire, and although after taking refuge in it the police had a most uncomfortable time from the heat and smoke coming from the main building, they refused to yield. At six o'clock, with the supply of rifle ammunition on our side running low and the possibility of reinforcements coming at any time, despite, the fact that the roads leading to Hollyford were all well barricaded by the Volunteers in the surrounding districts, the order to retire was given.

Séumas Robinson, as Brigade OC, weighed up all options and took the decision to call off the attack. A victory of sorts, however, did go to the Volunteers as the British forces who came to Hollyford evacuated the RIC from the barracks. Men from the local company then demolished what remained of the building. The withdrawal of the RIC from Hollyford was a big advantage to the IRA as it gave a great stretch of open country without any enemy posts located in it.

This attack was a watershed moment in the area. Although previous attempts on destroying enemy posts had been tried, Hollyford proved that a positive outcome could be achieved and that the IRA was capable of sustaining a prolonged attacked with their limited resources. With courage, determination and ingenuity, an attack could be pressed home.

Lessons were drawn that would help shape future operations. Excluding those engaged in road blocking and scouting duties, 63 men from the local Battalion, together with the Battalion Staff, took part in that attack on Hollyford Barracks. Those not required for the firing parties around the barracks were holding the ladder in position, drawing oil in buckets from the creamery and carrying the buckets of oil up the ladder to Robinson and O'Malley on the roof. Neither side had any casualties that night, but the IRA did glean valuable experience which they would soon put to good use.

Following from Hollyford, a series of coordinated attacks on a number of barracks was planned. The IRA in the area was growing in confidence and ambition. Robinson felt that they would adopt similar tactics but needed to feed the flames of the roof fire with more intensity than could be provided by buckets. Some sort of pump and hose would be used. Once again Robinson and O'Malley would mount the rooftop, and Treacy would command the ground operation.

Towards the end of May, instructions were issued by Robinson to the local Battalion that covered the area where Drangan Barracks was located, putting them on alert. They were to block the roads between Dualla to Drangan, and between Cashel and Fethard, on the night of 4 June, and for parties of armed Volunteers to be placed on the road-blocks.

At a later meeting, Séumas Robinson asked Battalion Staff members Paddy Hogan and Ed Grogan if they could obtain a hose in Cashel which, he explained, would be required for pumping paraffin oil on to the roof of the barracks. On the evening of 3 June, Hogan, Grogan and Tom Taylor took a hose from Cashel Railway Station and brought it to Drangan, leaving it at a house on Parsonshill.

It is approximately 18 miles from Cashel to Drangan and, to get there for the attack, the Volunteers borrowed a motor car from a sympathiser in Cashel. The car was driven by Dan Taylor. He had very limited experience of driving and, when they were within about a mile of Drangan, the car crashed into a ditch at the side of the road and was damaged. All four occupants were fortunate to escape injury, and continued their journey on foot.

Scouts whom they met on the road directed them on towards Drangan. They were given a box of home-made bombs to bring along. It was near midnight when they reached the village, and the attack was already under way. They went with the bombs to a bicycle repair shop which was situated next door to the barracks. Ernie O'Malley, Séumas Robinson, Seán Treacy and Tommy Donovan, Commandant of the 7th Battalion, were using it as a command post.

Parties of Volunteers, from positions at the front and rear of the barracks, were firing intermittently at the garrison, and the police were replying vigorously to their fire. Grogan recalled leaving his rifle to be used by some of the men on the road blocks. The only arms he had was a Webley revolver, so Séumas Robinson posted him at the door of the shop, with instructions to fire on any of the RIC who might attempt to leave the barracks by the front door.

Mud bombs, concocted by Seán Treacy, were flung on to the slated roof of the barracks. The wet clay adhered to the roof, and, as these improvised devices exploded, they tore holes in the slates. Grogan recounted:

> The next thing that I noticed was that Séumas Robinson had gone on to the roof of the barracks, and that Tommy

Donovan had started to work a hand-pump which pumped paraffin oil from a barrel on the floor of the bicycle repair shop on to the roof of the barracks. The hose from the pump led through a hole in the roof of the cycle repair shop and extended on to the roof of the barracks. A light pole was attached to that portion of the hose which played over the barrack roof to keep it steady and to direct the nozzle of the hose on to the part of the roof furthest from the shop.

In further recollections, Grogan remembered that this pole became detached from the hose and crashed to the street, straight in front of the barracks. He recovered it, after Ernie O'Malley shouted, "'We must get that pole back.'"

Towards daybreak, the roof of the barracks was burning fiercely; the police surrendered and gave up their arms. Immediately after the surrender, Ernie O'Malley and some Volunteers went into the barracks to search for any arms, ammunition or grenades which might still be there. They found one large wooden box of .303 ammunition and, as they carried it out, a piece of a burning rafter fell and hit O'Malley on the back of the neck. It gave him a pretty nasty burn. One of the police, a Black and Tan, had a slight wound over his right eye. He received first-aid from the IRA.

Séumas Robinson and Ernie O'Malley once again had played a hazardous role, with O'Malley recalling:

My face was blistered and sore and I could smell my burning hair. When I looked at Séumas I could not help laughing, for he had a halo of fire on his tufted head and shadow lights played on his face which was the cross between a bruised prize fighter and that of a chimney sweep.

When it came to dispersing, Grogan informed Séumas Robinson about the car crashing. He mentioned they had no way, except for walking, of getting back to Cashel. Robinson said, "'Take the first bicycle you meet.'" Grogan did, and took a bicycle which was left leaning against a wall, about 100 yards from the barracks. With one of the captured rifles tied to it, he cycled towards home and subsequently discovered that it was Robinson's own bicycle that he had taken!

Other attacks were planned throughout 1920. Seán Treacy and Jerome Davin prepared plans for an attack on Clerihan Barracks. They selected the positions to be occupied and the house from which the attack on the roof of the barracks would be made. Treacy arranged with the other Battalions to send men to Clerihan and for the blocking of all roads leading to the village on the appointed night.

The strength of the RIC garrison in Clerihan was one Sergeant and eleven Constables. As it was the nearest enemy post to Rosegreen, where the Brigade Headquarters was situated, the IRA were particularly keen to get rid of it and free up more countryside. It was situated between four British Garrison Towns; Clonmel being 4 miles away, Fethard 5 miles, and Cashel and Cahir approximately 8 miles each. Treacy felt that it would be an act of defiance and a blow to the prestige of the British forces in these towns if they succeeded in taking the barracks.

Davin believed 'that the capture of the barracks itself was as easy as cracking a nutshell. Our main concern was to hold off the British Troops if they came out from any of the four [garrison] towns, and thus it was that the intensive blocking of the roads and the manning of the road blocks was so important.'

On the appointed night the IRA went to Clerihan just after dark. Every detail was fully organised. They had a pump capable of propelling oil and petrol up to a distance of 60 yards. A load of yellow clay was brought in a horse drawn cart. They intended to make mud bombs on the spot. Milk churns were used as containers for the paraffin oil. The riflemen and shotgunmen took up positions around the barracks. Treacy and Davin then made a final check-up:

> Seán had a look at the barracks and at the house which I had decided we should occupy. He agreed that it was suitable as our key point of attack. It was at this point that Séumas Robinson, the Brigade O/C, arrived on the scene. He had just returned from Dublin. We told him everything was ready to go ahead with the attack. He told us that, in view of a recent G.H.Q. order, plans for major engagements, including attacks on barracks, would first have to be submitted to G.H.Q. for sanction. There was no alternative but to call off the attack. He was very definite that this G.H.Q. instruction should not be broken. Some of the Officers present, including Ned O'Reilly and myself, were sorely disappointed: but Seán Treacy, in his cool, calm manner, gave us an example in discipline, He simply remarked: "All right, Séumas, you are the boss."

Desmond Ryan in his book recorded that Treacy failed to mention that he had first received the order and then showed it to Robinson who subsequently castigated him for giving him the dispatch before the attack commenced. "'Why the Dickens,' he asked Treacy, "didn't you hold back that dispatch and let the attack go ahead?'"

British raids intensified in the area. A famous incident occurred that would later become known as 'The Blackcastle Races' when a Brigade Council meeting was surrounded by a group of British Lancers. One of the IRA guards managed to close a gate which forced the Lancers to dismount their horses, giving the officers valuable time to gather their papers and weapons before scattering. Exchanges of fire resulted in confusion, and Séumas Robinson was nearly intercepted by a group of soldiers. He ran past them and dove into a nearby pond and in the happy phrase of one present he 'became a submarine.' Sinking under the water Robinson placed a reed in his mouth to breathe and waited on the bewildered soldiers to disappear. This raid could have had disastrous consequences, but fortunately for the IRA all officers and men escaped.

Reprisals became an official response by the British forces in the aftermath of ambushes in a given locality or when men or materials were captured in people's homes. Robinson, ever conscious of the need for the IRA to maintain the support of the people, did not want the intended effect of the reprisals – namely, to drive fear into the civilian population and thus discourage active support – to come to fruition. Indeed, the reprisal policy had already caused Éamon Ó Duibhir to question IRA tactics, and he resigned because he felt 'the enemy's way of burning is a knockout blow to active service.'

About midsummer of 1920 Robinson issued an instruction to the Brigade that Volunteers caught inside houses where civilians were living should not fire until they were outside the house:

This was not an order because circumstances might arise where the Volunteers would have no alternative. I had had occasion to note that some very good Volunteers thought that the civilian population was at best only a secondary consideration. One night (I think it was when I went to Dublin to investigate the tragic Fernside affair and the consequent death of Professor Carolan and Seán Treacy) three of us were in The Monument Creamery in Camden Street when about 5 a.m. we were awakened by Tans and, or, Auxies, breaking into the rear of the whole block of buildings... When they started to break into the back of the

Creamery, I said that we had better get out to the back so that the British wouldn't know which house we had come out of, and fight our way out. Mick Sheehan who was extremely brave but devoid of much imagination insisted that it was our duty to defend ourselves by taking any and every advantage and therefore we should stay inside and fight it out from inside the house. I cut the argument short: "We'll get outside first!" Luckily, they did not search any of the houses: they were looking for some motor car, possibly the one we had come to Dublin in but it had returned to Tipperary.

This order was easier said than done, and as alternatives Robinson commissioned his Brigade Engineers to come up with a series of concealed hideaways that became known as 'Dug Outs.' Robinson outlined that:

> ...the principal reason for the dug-out policy was that it was unfair to the harassed civil population, whom it was our duty to protect and comfort, to have armed men in their homes who were determined if trapped in the house, to fight their way out. It was very nerve-racking to civilians to have us sleeping under their roofs, especially if there were children [inside]...

Five 'Dug Outs' were made. Jerome Davin noted that they used them as follows:

> (1) For use as Brigade Headquarters. This dug-out was used principally as an office by the Brigade Staff. Sleeping accommodation was provided in it by folding beds. It was electrically lit from batteries. When it was completed, we allocated 20 men from "A" Company as a special unit attached to the Brigade for dispatch and escort work.

(2) For use as Headquarters of the Battalion.

(3) "A" Company dug-out where up to 60 men could parade.

(4) One at Springfield which was used to hold prisoners.

(5) One which was used as an arms dump.

These dug-outs were never discovered by the British, although during one particular round-up, held in the early hours of the morning, troops actually walked over one of them whilst eleven men slept underneath.

The 'Dug-Out' utilised as Brigade HQ was located in a field near the Davin family home at Rathsallagh. It was always referred to as 'No. 71,' called after the address in Heytesbury Street, Dublin, where Séumas Robinson's fiancée lived. This field was screened by two high boundary ditches. The ground around it was strewn with stones and rubble which ensured that no footprints were left on the approach to the entrance. When Ernie O'Malley was taken to the dug-out he failed to find the access point, even though he was standing next to it.

Dispatch riders were not permitted to go to the Brigade HQ, nor were they familiar with its location. Instead, a central point was established where they brought the dispatches to a cowshed on a farm owned by people named O'Donnell of Tilloon near Rockwell College. This cowshed was situated about one mile from the main road, and here the dispatches were collected each day by Staff Officer Seán O'Meara and brought to Headquarters. Towards the end of 1920 the British were very active, raiding continuously, especially at night and always in large force. They would slow up their Crossley Tender lorries and some soldiers would drop out, lying in ambush for whatever would come along. Robinson noticed that the lorries seemed to break down fairly frequently and on enquiring from his Engineering Department, learned that Crossley Tenders were very vulnerable in their axels. The roads in Tipperary had not been repaired for quite some time. Robinson ensured that the pot-holes took a heavy toll on the Crossleys:

> It is easy to guess that it struck me that if we increased the number of pot-holes it would be to our advantage. I thought it well to ask G.H.Q's permission and at the same time they could take the hint to spread the idea further if they approved ... and I couldn't think of any reason why we shouldn't be allowed to go ahead. But G.H.Q. replied after about a week that the Department of Local Government would not sanction "the destruction of the people's property." This was the first time G.H.Q. had given any reason for their decisions in a dispatch, and that, taken in conjunction with the delay in answering led me to think that G.H.Q. was not pleased with this Government decision…
> I do remember that I got round the difficulty by issuing a Brigade order to all Companies to enlarge the existing potholes!

Perhaps the biggest setback to the war effort in Tipperary happened not in the county but in the streets of Dublin with the death of Seán Treacy after a shootout in Talbot Street. Treacy had gone to the capital to finalise arrangements for his pending marriage to May Quigley. She was working in Dublin at that time but was transferring jobs to County Clare.

Treacy billeted with Dan Breen. The conflict in Dublin had become much more intense; it was a dangerous place for wanted men. They moved to a different safe house in Drumcondra but had been shadowed by British Intelligence agents. A surprise raid was carried out in the early hours of the morning and the two IRA men managed to fight their way out. Breen was injured after dropping from an upper floor through a green house. He was brought to the Mater Hospital for treatment and while there the British began raiding the hospital. Not wanting his comrade captured Treacy at once sprang into action and went to Peadar Clancy's shop in Talbot Street to mobilise some men for a rescue party.

Unfortunately for Treacy, the shop was under surveillance and the Intelligence Agents pounced. He was shot dead as he returned fire, mortally wounding Lieutenant Price. About an hour beforehand Treacy had a meal at 71 Heytesbury Street. Brigid Keating was probably the last person to see him alive and she would later help to identify his body.

Séumas Robinson would feel the loss keenly; not only had he lost a close friend and comrade but also his most able organiser. He wrote 'when Seán was killed in Talbot Street, Dublin, I found it a wholetime job to attend to the organisation (which was Treacy's work as Vice O/C) of the Brigade and the activities of the Columns from a centre which, though constantly raided, had to continue to carry on as a co-ordinating point.'

Robinson asked Jerome Davin to go to Tipperary Town and to make the funeral arrangements for Treacy. A large force of British military was present at Limerick Junction when the train bringing his remains arrived. Davin remembered that 'I must say that on that particular night they [the British] certainly were not aggressive. As a matter of fact, a party of them presented arms as the coffin covered with the tricolour was borne from the train to the hearse.'

From Limerick Junction to the church at Solohead the route was lined by British soldiers, but they did not deter thousands of people, including many Volunteers, from marching behind the hearse. Next day when the burial took place British troops were again present in and around the cemetery at Kilfeacle, they harrassed mourners and seized some bicycles which were left around by their owners. The officer withdrew the military before the grave was fully filled in and there was no interference with the firing party who subsequently fired the three volleys with revolvers.

Davin also felt the death of Treacy deeply and lamented that 'To my mind Seán Treacy's death was the biggest blow the Third Tipperary Brigade could or did receive. His personality commanded respect, and during the years I was associated with him only on one or two occasions did I ever see him perturbed or impatient…'

The Volunteers of South Tipperary had no time to mourn the loss of Treacy; they still had a war to fight. Almost immediately following Treacy's death, the Columns were formed and the whole energies of the best fighting men were concentrated on the operations and activities of these special units. Thomas Ryan, a member of No. 2 Column recorded:

The activities of the Brigade Staff from then on became almost purely administrative, giving support to the Columns by intelligence and communication services. From the time the Columns began operations, Robinson remained in and about the Brigade Headquarters at Rosegreen, taking no active part in the work of the Columns, and so was not regarded by the men of the Columns as having any effective control of them. In fact, the Column Commanders at this time seemed to be supreme in their respective commands, the Brigade Headquarters merely acting as a centre for intelligence reports and other communications. From this, it may be seen that we looked upon Robinson's position as Brigade Commander as purely nominal, though, with the wisdom of later years, I realise that, had he been possessed of a more forceful character and spent most of his time with the Columns where he might have influenced or directed their activities on the spot, we might have had less to lament in the way of lost opportunities.

Two Flying Columns were formed in the area. No.1 Column under the command of Dinny Lacey and the other headed up by Seán Hogan. Robinson, in fact, wanted Thomas Ryan to lead the column, but Ryan did not want to take the position. He remembered his exchange with Séumas Robinson on the matter:

The fact that I would not consent to become Flying Column Commander was a disappointment to the Company Commanders who gave me their enthusiastic support. The Brigade Commander, Séumas Robinson, also expressed his disappointment that I would not accept command of the Column. I had suggested Seán Hogan for this appointment because Hogan had indicated to me that he was willing and even anxious to be appointed as Column Commander. I was invited by the Brigade Commander to attend at Brigade Headquarters which was at Rosegreen. It was there that I discussed this matter of the appointment of a Column Commander with Séumas Robinson. Seán O'Meara was present with Robinson when I went to Brigade Headquarters. Robinson asked me what was the idea of inviting Hogan to take command of the Battalion and the Column. I told him that I felt that Hogan was more capable than I of carrying out the duties of such an appointment... Robinson, however, knew Hogan rather better than I did, and his remarks to me on this occasion showed his wisdom. He said, "If you insist in handing over the Battalion to Hogan, you will regret it." I could not see any reason why I should ever regret such a thing at the time, and so Hogan was appointed to the command of the 6th Battalion. Fighting as an individual for Ireland meant everything to me, rank and command meant nothing. The chief argument Robinson made against Hogan's appointment was that he considered him too young for the job. At any rate, he was appointed.

The two Flying Columns began operating in South Tipperary with mixed success. Lacey in particular proved to be an astute commander and would eventually succeed Robinson as Brigade OC when the latter was appointed to the new position of Divisional Commander in succession to Ernie O'Malley in late 1921.

Soon, Ryan regretted not taking heed of Robinson and by-passing the opportunity to take command of the Column. After one particularly lucky escape he remembered that there was open talk amongst the men about replacing Hogan:

> At this time, a number of us were very dissatisfied with Hogan's leadership. There were about 12 or 14 of the Column who wanted me to take over the leadership because they felt that Hogan was lacking in common-sense and we were tired of being continuously hunted. Being surrounded every now and again and getting out of these difficulties more by good luck than good generalship had a demoralising effect on the Column, and we wanted to take the initiative in action of our own making. Hogan's attitude appeared to be that, so long as the Column continued to exist and did not lose any men or arms, it continued to be a thorn in the side of the enemy and so served its purpose. But a number of us had different views and wanted to take more positive action.

Despite the mixed successes of the Columns, Robinson felt they had served their purpose and he noted that:

By '21 we had the area cleared of all small enemy posts, and the larger Columns became cumbersome, so I decided to break up the Columns into Battalion Columns so that a greater amount of smaller activities could take place. The smaller the target we presented to the enemy the safer for us. Big operations were impossible and dangerous and what the enemy would have liked.

Violence was an everyday occurrence; fear, terror and suspicion were ever-present. The British continued to use reprisals, many homes and businesses were destroyed including Kilshenane. Spies and informers were utilised in the efforts against the IRA. Robinson remembered one particular case of a man who called himself 'O'Neill.' He denied being an agent during questioning and stated that he was in the locality looking for work. He had no form of identification, which the IRA felt was suspicious in itself. All he possessed was an ornamental clip of ammunition. Séumas Robinson explained:

Then Jerome Davin, O/C. Bn. 1, shot a bow at a venture: "This ornamental clip gives you away completely." "That's only a souvenir." "Yes! Well the last spy we shot told us before he died that it was a secret identification among Intelligence Agents." "Oh! The dirty, mean, dastardly, cowardly bastard." I don't guarantee the order of the adjectives he used but he used them all and more; but he did not use in my presence any of the usual filthy British Army lingo. He was a Catholic and Fr. Kingston of Rockwell College attended him the night he was executed. Just as he was about to be shot, he made one last dramatic outburst of denial that he was a spy. I went over to him and said quietly: "Young man, you are about to die. Don't say anything that may sully your conscience at this awful moment." Instantly he had himself under control. "I'm not afraid to die" was all he answered.

The year 1921 was to be a significant year for Séumas Robinson and his comrades. Violence was reaching a climax and unbeknown to the people at large an end was in sight. The IRA would see significant highs with the calling of a Truce but ultimately the year would end with a great schism within the ranks of the Republican Movement.

CHAPTER EIGHT

TORN UP FOR BANDAGES

Truce, Treaty and Civil War: Ireland 1921 -1923

Early in 1921 Liam Lynch, OC Second Cork Brigade IRA, asked Séumas Robinson to attend a meeting in Cork to discuss the pros and cons of co-operation among their respective Brigades. The Cork delegates, including Liam Lynch, insisted that Robinson chaired the meeting. Con Moloney, who was Robinson's Adjutant, was asked to act as Secretary. Within an hour of holding discussions they had the headings for a report to GHQ in reference to forming an IRA Division.

The reason for suggesting the formation of a larger command area was that enemy posts were now supersized and concentrated in the larger towns, effectively putting them beyond the reach of the IRA in their current structure. GHQ initially turned down their suggestion, but later adopted it by dividing the proposed divisional area into two, thus forming the First and Second Southern Divisions. Liam Lynch was given command of the First Southern Division, while Ernie O'Malley was appointed Officer Commanding of the Second Southern Division which incorporated South Tipperary. This was around April 1921. It was quite evident that GHQ did not want an 'autonomous freelancer' like Robinson to be in charge of a larger and more influential command. They, therefore, appointed whom they believed to be two trusted officers.

Robinson stated that the origin of the idea of forming the Army into larger divisions arose incidentally to, and developed subsequently during, a 'dispute' between him and Lynch. And the above-mentioned meeting was part of the process to reach a resolution. Robinson outlined the context:

> Early in October, 1920 (as the war was rapidly rising to a crescendo of violence and the British were systematically bringing to perfection their tactics of sudden mass concentrations of scattered forces for large-scale round-ups), Liam Lynch travelled to Davin's of Rathsallagh, near Cashel, (our Brigade Headquarters) and complained with what seemed to me to be a good deal of pent-up feeling and politely-suppressed indignation that the South Irish Horse (a British Cavalry Unit stationed at Cahir Military Barracks) was continually raiding southwards into his Brigade area. He informed me in measured terms that it was my bounden duty as the O/C of the area in which Cahir was situated, to put an instant stop to these irksome, disconcerting raids - by sealing them off from the South. I told him that these same S.I.H. had been doing the same thing north, east and west into our territories from 1918 until a few months previously when they gave up coming our way because they had got nothing but headaches from us. "They must be finding it less uncongenial to raid Cork 2", I badgered in the good-humoured banter we all inflicted on one another in those days, especially if there was even a slight danger of a debate degenerating into argument. But Lynch was deadly serious. Liam was ever a man in a hurry to get something done. I had come to know many, if not most, of his idiosyncrasies.

Robinson did know Liam Lynch well. When Lynch visited Dublin, on-the-run from 1919, he always had his private hide-

187

out at the Tipperary Brigade's Dublin Headquarters in 71 Heytesbury Street. Robinson remembered:

> I got to know how seriously Liam viewed everything. I felt that he ignored if not deliberately suppressed, as a waste of time and energy, his own sense of humour. Yet he must have developed a good sense of humour. No man could possibly have lived and worked so long and so much with so many of the Cork boys without being smitten by a reasonable dose of their contagion.

Soberly, Robinson pointed out to Lynch that if the Third Tipperary Brigade attempted to deal with the problem of the Southern Irish Horse in the way he had suggested, they would have to keep a very large and well-armed force permanently isolated in the narrow Aherlow Glen. Logistically they would be hemmed in between large British forces situated in Kilworth Camp and Mallow in the south and Cahir and Clonmel in the north and, at the same time, hedged in by the Galtee and Knockmealdown Mountains in the west and east.

Robinson laid emphasis on the fact that neither his Brigade nor indeed any other IRA Brigade had the equipment necessary or the numbers to spare, and that his Brigade had neither the inclination nor any intention to attempt such a suicidal commitment. The Glen of Aherlow was constantly being searched by combined British forces from Cork, Waterford and Tipperary. Seán Hogan's Column, for example, escaped on one occasion during one of these enormous concentrations only by a miracle of coolness. Dinny Lacey's column captured District Inspector Potter in the process of fighting its way out on another occasion.

Liam Lynch recognised these difficulties. According to Robinson 'I think he [Lynch] sensed the latent hint that this particular cap fitted more than one head. Nevertheless, it did not absolve me in his eyes. "You will have to do something about it," he insisted.'

Robinson wanted to invoke some corporate responsibility and come up with a shared solution:

Knowing Liam's penchant (probably G.H.Q. engendered) for paper organisation and knowing how wasteful of critical time it could be with so many unforeseeable factors involved, I made the obvious suggestion that the only possible way to deal with the situation was to combine at once sufficient forces on lines parallel to the British. Liam murmured it would be necessary to get permission from G.H.Q. before making even a tentative change in Army formation. I had suggested a try-out combination on a voluntary basis among a number of local Brigades. We could begin with an association of the three Cork Brigades, East Limerick Brigade and the 2nd and 3rd Tipperary Brigades. These six Brigades were all of a timbre. They were contiguous. The slight psychological differences among us were complementary rather than divergent. There would be a mixture of different kinds of good milk, but there would be no addition of water in the mixture. They would make an almost irresistible force. They were all of good will, keen; they all had the practical experience necessary for larger combinations. They could be augmented as necessity or opportunity arose.

The IRA in the field was becoming more ambitious. As the war progressed, men like Robinson and Lynch saw the need to adopt their tactics and respond to the evolving operational methods being utilised by the British. In order for the IRA to be effective, they needed to pool their resources and attempt something more ambitious to counteract their enemy and regain the military initiative. Robinson continued:

As the piece-de-resistance for Liam, I harped on about the immediate necessity of liquidating (though that word was not much used among us then) Cahir Military Barracks. As an initial test, it had much to recommend it. If successful, even if the success were only relative, we should then have concrete demonstrable proof of the value and necessity of combining Brigades for super-brigade actions. The necessity of combining Brigades should have been self-evident even to our G.H.Q. hidden (and rightly so) in the fortresses of their Dublin dug-outs. Their only vision was the reflection of the City activities. It was only after de Valera's return from the U.S.A. that the attack on the Custom House was mooted. They could not focus large-scale operations.

At that time Robinson thought that GHQ would have been delighted to see such a spirit of initiative coming from the field. He gathered from brief hints from Lynch that he would prefer to start with all Munster and that they should not initiate anything without prior permission from GHQ. 'In fairness to Liam it must be added that that attitude seemed to please G.H.Q.!' Robinson's lack of confidence in and growing suspicion of GHQ and their motives was becoming more evident:

On the other hand, it was my conviction that, during revolutionary periods, if a thing be morally right in itself and at the same time be urgent and necessary, it would be legitimatized subsequently - for what pure legalities are worth in a revolution with the enemy taking full advantage of our slow moving, hobble skirted Army formation and regulations! Here were we lying in wait for permission to surprise the enemy with a new tactic while he was all ready and afoot to attack us. It would have taken a truce of three months' duration to enable us to organise all Munster into a unified fighting force by any other means than by concrete example. Example would bring in every unit automatically and instantly. I think Liam imagined I was inviting him to put the telescope to a blind eye - which he had not got. At best he must have suspected that I was handing him the wrong end of a telescope to look through. Liam must have got the low-down on me from G.H.Q.! It was well known to me and to other Brigade Officers that G.H.Q. was Sanctum Sanctorum to Man, that the Chief of Staff was its High Priest, and that Liam and all Cork were as the children of light to G.H.Q. And rightly so. As a County, no place was doing as much; as a man, no one had done more than Liam Lynch to break the British connection. This is not an "admission" on my part. "Admission" savours of reluctance to say a thing: I have no reluctance whatever to declaring, no apology to offer for saying as I now repeat, that Liam Lynch and all Rebel Cork were outstanding and were deservedly courted by G.H.Q.

Robinson recalled that Lynch was quietly fidgeting with obvious impatience at what must have seemed to him, at any rate, the 'dialectics' being articulated. Capturing Lynch's personality Robinson recorded that:

...in his usual quiet, strictly polite manner, his intriguing slight impediment of speech a little accentuated, he put his proposition direct, unequivocally and with finality: "Will I call a meeting of Munster Brigade Officers, get their views and send a report to G.H.Q.?" What else could I do but take his hand, shake it warmly and say: "I'm behind you, Liam."

Liam Lynch lost no time in calling the meetings. They were held in Glanworth, County, Cork. Most of the Munster Brigades East of the Shannon were represented. IRA veteran Florrie O'Donoghue, in his biography of Lynch, records the details of their discussions. There was complete unanimity. The report was duly forwarded to GHQ who subsequently, and without any acknowledgement reaching Robinson as Chairperson, informed them through Ernie O'Malley (who had not been at the meeting) that Munster was to be divided into four separate Divisions.

Robinson was angered by this development and believed that both the Rebel and the Premier Counties were isolated anew and more effectively by this less ambitious move. Cahir Barracks was never seriously attacked and, now on paper, the country as a whole was divided into Sixteen IRA Divisions. Robinson asked:

> Was it method in their madness or was it madness in their method that killed a scheme that would have borne quick fruit? Perhaps G.H.Q. were aware of the beginnings of peace negotiations about that time, and perhaps the Chief of Staff wanted to be able to say (as he said later), with some semblance of conviction, that "The I.R.A. could not attack a reasonably sized Police Barracks." (Dáil reports, December, 1921).

Robinson's relationship with GHQ already strained, would deteriorate further. The Dublin reaction to Soloheadbeg solidified his dual suspicion of what he termed the influence of 'Sinn Féin pacificism' and 'the sinister cabal' of the IRB. These feelings between Robinson and many of the Dublin based leadership seem to have been mutual. This distrustful outlook held by Séumas Robinson was noted by Ernie O'Malley, who was to administer the oath of allegiance to the Dáil amongst the South Tipperary IRA:

Séumas was opposed to it. "Why doesn't the Volunteer Executive call a Convention to consider such an important step? The Dáil might go wrong" he said, "it might accept something less than a Republic…" Seán [Treacy] and I laughed. "I suppose GHQ might go wrong also?" asked Seán. "Yes, it might." We laughed again. He looked at us very sombrely with a dour expression in his brown eyes and a pursing of his stubborn underlip. He dissected things too much we thought. He analysed orders and sought motives. Mulcahy and Collins admired him but they did not like him.

Little did they realise then that Robinson's thoughts would be prophetic. Todd Andrews noted that 'Many personal antipathies suppressed for the cause were soon to break out in sores and festered with surprising rapidity in the lead up to the Civil War.'

Perhaps in an effort to counter 'dyed in the wool pacifists' another significant development took place in 1921 with the election of Séumas Robinson to the Second Dáil as the TD for East Tipperary and Waterford.

Some controversy arose in the Tipperary constituency with Séumas Robinson taking the nomination instead of the preferred Sinn Féin candidate, Brigid Dooley. Robinson mentions that 'In 1921 the Volunteers asked me to stand for election to the Second Dáil, and I was elected for East Tipperary and Waterford in the place of the late Pierce McCan.' The standing committee of Sinn Féin was dissatisfied with the nomination but could do very little. As late as nomination day, Dooley was listed as the candidate 'so her replacement was obviously a last-minute affair, but here too, headquarters was unable to influence the decisions of locally dominant Volunteers' according to historian Michael Laffin.

This move would place Séumas Robinson in the midst of the coming controversy around the Anglo-Irish Treaty. He would be in the public eye of the storm as a member of Dáil Éireann.

The war had reached a climax; Ireland, in effect, had become ungovernable for the British. Peace feelers had been extended, and soon a Truce came into effect during the summer of 1921. Dispatches from GHQ ordered that all hostilities would cease at 12 noon on 11 July. IRA officers like Robinson and O'Malley believed that this would be a temporary affair and the IRA should take full advantage of the breathing space presented to them to take stock, retrain, recruit and review their tactics given that they could now move about freely.

British Intelligence noted that South Tipperary during the Truce period was 'actually making preparations in every way for a renewal of disturbance should the negotiations not be successful... in parts of Tipperary rebels have utilised the Truce to reorganise, refit and establish training camps.' Indeed, they even noted correspondence that Séumas Robinson had with his mother, where he informed her about his regret that a Truce had been called and he expressed a willingness to restart hostilities again if necessary.

The Truce conferred considerable prestige and legitimacy upon the IRA. O'Malley saw a danger in this and observed:

> The Irish Republican Army was in danger of becoming popular, recruits came in large numbers... we had to give officers sufficient work to keep them busy and do our best to prevent them from entering towns and cities where they would become known to enemy intelligence agents.

From a GHQ perspective, the South Tipperary Brigade was not strictly observing the terms of truce. Two RIC men were shot in

Cashel in December just as the negotiations were reaching a critical point. The most serious incident, however, proved to be a raid for arms on a British Army barracks in Tipperary Town. Over 70 rifles and a machine gun were seized. Both the British and IRA GHQ were fuming. A wall of silence enveloped the Brigade, and all officers were summoned to Dublin. Not for the first time, Séumas Robinson was summoned to GHQ for questioning and reprimand.

Ernie O'Malley recorded what happened after Con Molony, adjutant of the Second Southern Division, emerged from his GHQ interview:

> Séumas Robinson asked "Well Con, what penance did you get?" … We looked like a group waiting for confession. Con's blue eyes twinkled. "Collins is in a hell of a rage" he said. "Watch my poker face." Finally, Collins completely lost his temper, he was keenly aware the impact the raid could have on the negotiations in London. "Come on by Christ and answer the questions I ask." His voice became threatening. "We're not going to let you get away with those lousy rifles." The Tipperary officers remained silent and Collins stormed out. There was silence for a moment. Then we laughed.

In the new reality facing them, the British were now concentrated in large garrisons. The Divisional idea had been an attempt to address this, but Robinson also saw the need to procure the necessary hardware that would allow them to attack these strongholds. He believed that GHQ had not been forthcoming with sourcing the right equipment and he was quite critical of the role GHQ had played in supplying the Brigades with arms. Robinson had previously attempted to get one GHQ operative to work exclusively for him, but Bob Briscoe had politely refused.

His quest for arms knew no bounds, and he asked Roddy Connolly, son of the late James Connolly, for his help in sourcing 'procurement agents.' Utilising his contacts in the various Communist Parties, Connolly obtained false passports for agents to travel on arms procurement missions throughout Europe, which, in the aftermath of the Great War, was awash with weaponry. Two unlikely figures, the Beaumont brothers, set off on respective missions. One, Billy, was an ex-British army officer who tried to purchase Minenwerfer and anti-tank guns in Germany, but to no avail. While the other, Seán, went to Moscow to appeal for weapons, but the fledgling Comintern refused to entertain him. Due to these connections, Robinson was to gain a lifetime reputation as being 'close to the Reds.' He was also described as being left-wing and a 'Social Republican.' Some press outlets during the Civil War would also refer to Tipperary disparagingly as the home of 'Red Republicanism' and would single out Séumas Robinson in particular as a 'Bolshevik with a penchant for burning private property.' Jokingly, he would call this 'improperganda.'

With the conclusion of negotiations, a Treaty was signed in London agreeing the creation of the Irish Free State and granting Dominion Status to 26 of Ireland's 32 counties. A separate unionist political entity had effectively been created in the six north eastern counties. Ireland was partitioned, would remain a part of the British Empire and would be subservient to Westminster with all political representatives swearing an oath of allegiance to the Crown.

This was anathema to many Republicans. A spilt between Pro and Anti-Treaty positions emerged which spanned both the political and military sides of the Movement. From an Army perspective most of GHQ and the Chief of Staff, Richard Mulcahy, were promoting support for the Treaty while many Brigades were leaning towards opposing it. Ernie O'Malley remembered:

Séumas Robinson was dogged. His hair was tousled. He had his clenched fist underneath his underlip. Somehow, he had sensed that one day something would go wrong. There was an old antagonism between Mulcahy and himself. Séumas had too much of the French kind of inquiring critical knowledge.

Éamon Ó Duibhir in this period worked feverishly to prevent Civil War. He was in Dublin to meet with Collins. Ó Duibhir noted Collins' comments; 'he said jocosely to me: "Éamon, do you know what was the worst thing you did in your life?" I told him I could not pick one out of the many, and then he said: "Bringing Séumas Robinson to Tipperary."'

Robinson, as a senior IRA officer, was involved in many discussions around the position of the Army. His own stance, which he would articulate publicly as a Dáil Deputy during the Treaty Debate, was that the IRA should not blindly follow the direction of GHQ, nor indeed the Dáil. Robinson felt that IRA Volunteers were Citizen Soldiers, motivated to fight by their political belief in an Irish Republic; thus, they had an incumbent duty to ensure that goal was achieved even if it meant breaking away from GHQ and the Dáil.

In the midst of all this crisis, one happy event did take place for Robinson. He married on 29 December 1921 in the University Church, St Stephen's Green. His bride was Cumann na mBan Volunteer Brigid Keating, from the famed 71 Heystesbury Street. John Dempsey, the sacristan of the church, recalled many years later that 'the Bridegroom wore guns,' not a usual occurrence at the many weddings that took place in the church during his tenure. Dan Breen acted as Best Man; this would probably be the last time the two men would share an amicable occasion together.

There would be no honeymoon period for Robinson as the Treaty Debates were in full swing. In one of the preliminary, private sittings of the Dáil, he gave a glimpse into his thinking and a clear indication of his position. As an IRA officer, he articulated that there was still merit in the use of physical force against Britain.

He felt that, 'Lloyd George had bluffed this country' with his threat of immediate and terrible war and that the IRA in the field could fight back and that they should increase their operations in England. He stated that '50 men in England would be able to counteract any destruction that the British could do because thanks to British oppression we are not a manufacturing country... England depends on her factories and shipyards and we could work more destruction on England than she could on us.'

He then went on to a thinly veiled attack on GHQ, accusing them of 'criminal negligence.' In a further swipe directed at the IRB, he predicted that the passing of the Treaty would be akin to the underhanded passage of the Act of Union.

'I remember somewhere of a "Black Book" in 1801. Possibly there will be a "Black Book" now.' Finally, Robinson concluded by asking will the IRA follow this new government? Answering, he firmly stated 'I know that I can speak at any rate for my own Brigade and I do not believe that they will ... I think, and I know, that many Volunteers will think that this new government will be ultra vires and will have no binding, moral, legal or any other weight with us.'

These private sessions were only a warm up. Public sessions would take place in early January 1922. Here, Dáil Deputies would have a platform and an audience; the fracture within the Republican Movement would be clear for all to see. From the beginning, Séumas Robinson was straight to the point. 'In my own plain, direct, if not too lucid way, I would like to fire a few shots at this Treaty – metaphorically speaking.'

To him, the Treaty was a betrayal of the Republic, and that everything would and should be done to uphold what was declared at Easter 1916. Robinson believed that, 'The Republic is at stake and I don't give a rap whose reputation is torn up for bandages.' This compromise, he believed, had a long gestation and became 'a chrysalis when Dublin HQ became a wage-earning business' that sought through paid district commands 'to control men who fought the war, aye, and won it without any appreciable assistance from Dublin Headquarters.'

In Robinson's opinion, the Treaty represented a further humiliation to the downtrodden Irish people. If they accepted the terms of the Treaty, then the Dáil would not only let down Ireland but peoples all across the British Empire who 'have given us the sincerest form of flattery by imitating us.' The Treaty was not a secure foundation for peace, he likened it to a mule in that it was barren and should not be accepted under any circumstance as 'chaos would be better than degradation.'

He then proceeded to read a statement on behalf of a number of IRA officers voicing their opposition to the Treaty. Many Deputies felt this was a threat. Even de Valera, who was emerging as the arch political opponent of the Treaty criticised this intervention, but Robinson pressed ahead. He stated, with some justification, that 'If we had no political outlook, we would not be soldiers at all.' He articulated that the IRA was a people's army, called into being on a political issue to fight for a political cause. To pretend otherwise was to deny the very nature and raison d'être of the IRA. The Volunteers were Citizen Soldiers, motivated to fight by their ideals; they were the successors of Easter 1916 and guardians of the Republic.

The very fact that they were discussing a Treaty at all was not lost on Robinson. They were in this position due to the cutting edge of the IRA campaign. Not giving the IRA Volunteers a voice was, in his opinion, grossly unfair. As Citizen Soldiers, who had put their lives on the line, Séumas Robinson believed that the IRA should have a veto. 'We are not a national army in the ordinary sense… we have political views as soldiers. For the purpose of this veto I here demand a General Convention of the Volunteers who are not Truce Volunteers.'

It was clear that the reaction of the IRA to the Anglo-Irish Treaty would be crucial. The Volunteers had their own opinions and they didn't care if they would be at odds with the public mood. Ernie O'Malley believed that 'we never consulted the feelings of the people. If so, we would have never fired a shot. If we gave them a good, strong lead, they would follow.'

Many IRA activists felt that Séumas Robinson had eloquently articulated their stance. Todd Andrews was cheered by Robinson's speech:

> This totally expressed my feelings. I had never been happy with the oath of allegiance to Dáil Éireann. Having seen the Dáil in action, I was convinced that the only hope of realising the national objective was through the intervention of the Army.

Many within the IRA were suspicious of 'politics' and 'politicians,' viewing the art of compromise as something inherently wrong, something which their arms would have to rectify. Andrews also noted that since the days of The Irish Parliamentary Party the word 'politician' was never used to refer to Republicans:

> It was a word of ill repute. Now nearly all the members of the Dáil became, in my eyes, 'politicians.' A distinction was

rapidly being drawn between the 'politicians' and the 'army.' In the critical situation that was now developing my hopes were pinned on the unity of the IRA being maintained and, on the IRA, effectively taking over the institutions of government.

Séumas Robinson's speech was also notable for its attack on GHQ in general and Michael Collins in particular. A prevailing theme in many Pro-Treaty speeches was the mantle of 'what is good enough for Mick Collins is good enough for me.' Robinson went on the attack and stated that Collins's great deeds existed on paper only and he certainly was not the man who won the war. 'I am forced to think that the reported Michael Collins could not possibly be the same Michael Collins who was so weak as to compromise the Republic.'

Remaining unrepentant, Robinson wrote later in life that considerable propaganda surrounded Collins and related stories of his deeds and daring were simply not true. He reasoned this was done deliberately to put Collins on a pedestal, to win the hearts and minds of a war weary people and ensure that the compromise, weighted towards the British, contained within the Treaty, would be accepted:

> "What's good enough for Michael Collins is good enough for me" as I.R.B. Deputy after Deputy declared during the "Treaty" debates thereby renouncing his oath to the Republic, determined to swear (false?) fealty to his Satanic Majesty (excuse me), his Britannic Majesty. When he treacherously signed the Treaty, the anti-Republican press, to a sheet, were fulsome in their praise of Collins who they would have handed over to the British shortly before.

Robinson's long-held distrust and suspicion of the IRB was now vindicated in his eyes. He certainly was not impressed by the role played by the 'sinister cabal' in undermining the progress made towards establishing a Republic. The influence of the IRB was immense, but Robinson had consciously made the effort to minimise it in his command; indeed, Mulcahy bemoaned that the IRB influence did not extend to Robinson and his troublesome South Tipperary Brigade as 'persons such as Robinson had as little opinion of IRB activity as they had of GHQ.'

The Treaty went to a vote in the Dáil and was passed by a narrow margin of 62 to 57. Robinson pinpointed the dark influence of the IRB at work in ensuring that the outcome was in favour of Collins' position.

Séumas Robinson engaged with other prominent army officers about what they should do. The majority of IRA Brigades and Divisions were opposed to the Treaty and felt that both the authority of the Pro-Treaty GHQ and Dáil were no longer binding. The first Division to repudiate the authority of GHQ was the Second Southern Division under Ernie O'Malley in mid-January 1922. A significant driver of this move was Séumas Robinson who would soon succeed O'Malley as Divisional OC.

With purpose, Robinson toured his command area to ensure that no one took a Pro-Treaty position. Carlton Younger in his book on Ireland's Civil War concluded that Robinson's logic was 'Apart from the importance of unity he foresaw that men so familiar with the countryside would be dangerous in the event of Civil War.' One Pro-Treaty Volunteer, Thomas Ryan, stated that there was some initial support for the Treaty in South Tipperary but due to the influence of Séumas Robinson and Dinny Lacey many were persuaded to change their position. According to Ryan 'Both had been heroes during the Anglo-Irish War and a direct appeal from them swayed many into the Anti-Treaty ranks.' Ryan remained actively Pro-Treaty but had to leave Tipperary as Robinson was going to arrest him for recruiting 'Irish Black and Tans.'

Other Brigades and Units followed suit, and a General Army Convention was called for March 1922 which would formalise the split in the IRA. An Army Executive was formed which would take over command of what would now be termed the Anti-Treaty IRA. Séumas Robinson was elected to the Army Executive. He would play a prominent role in the unfolding events which would eventually create the circumstances where Civil War became inevitable.

Although Civil War seemed unavoidable, significant efforts were taken, nonetheless, to avert it. Brother killing brother seemed too high a price, so 'Army Unity' talks took place between Pro and Anti-Treaty officers. Robinson, as a member of the Executive, was involved in these talks. In the political arena talks were also held to create a 'Pact' for the forthcoming elections in an effort to avoid a formal split.

Running in conjunction with these efforts both sides were preparing militarily. Séumas Robinson, along with Joe McKelvey and Oscar Traynor, borrowed his mother-in-law's car and they left 71 Heytesbury Street and began to reconnoitre buildings in Dublin to decide on what positions to take over and to establish a General Headquarters; the taking over of the Four Courts was the result. They also identified strategic buildings all over the city and the IRA began to fortify positions. Robinson held the firm belief that control of Dublin was crucial.

As part of the 'Army Unity' talks, mentioned above, there was agreement that there would be a de-escalation in Dublin but the Four Courts would remain as the Army Executive Headquarters. Séumas Robinson felt that this move was premature and placed too much trust in Collins and Mulcahy. He was adamant in his arguments around the strategic importance of holding their positions in Dublin and ensuring their readiness to make a decisive strike.

Séumas Robinson represented the Executive on the actual taking over of the Four Courts; ably assisted by Seán Fitzpatrick's Tipperary Column and members of the Dublin Brigade. He was to remain here for around a week before going back to his command area where he began to forcibly stop the fledgling Free State Army from occupying any barracks. He did not want them having a foothold anywhere in his area.

'The Kilkenny and Limerick incidents brought about by the "Staters" not keeping their bargain to allow the local Volunteers, by majority, to take over vacated barracks. O'Malley came down to help uphold the honour of his old Division,' recalled Robinson. Civil War was nearly pre-empted in his area as disputes arose over the Free State Army trying to occupy positions. Robinson held firm, and his hard-line stance paid off dividends in the initial stages of the Civil War as his Divisional Lines proved difficult to penetrate.

In a blow to the Republican position, Robinson lost his seat in the Dáil at the 'Pact' elections. He felt that the agreement on which the elections was fought was never honoured by their opponents. The British Government, in particular Winston Churchill, was pushing Collins and the Free State Provisional Government to take decisive action against the IRA. This action soon took place. The Civil War would commence at the end of June 1922.

Séumas Robinson left the Four Courts at midnight on 27 June, the night before the attack by the Free State Army. He left after what he termed 'a whale of an argument with Liam Mellows and Rory O'Connor on the foolishness of the Headquarters of the

Army having all its eggs in the one basket.' There was no coherent strategy in place, and the Free State would take full advantage of this and make the first move.

Robinson escaped from the city on the afternoon of 28 June just as the Battle of Dublin was getting underway. He met Seán McSweeney and Liam Lynch on the train leaving for the South. There, Robinson recalled that they 'debated almost to argument the foolishness, as I thought it, of the policy of each Unit staying home in its own area' and engaging the Free State Army in the localities.

Meeting Lynch later in Clonmel, Séumas Robinson said that he again tried to convince 'Liam to command the whole Army, to march on Dublin and cut out the cancer before it spread.' He couldn't move Lynch from the notion of fighting in their localities:

> I didn't want another split, so I resigned. Lynch wouldn't hear of it. I told him how it felt in Easter Week when the country did not come to our aid; I explained that before I left [The Four Courts] I sent word to [Oscar] Traynor that my Division would be rushed to Dublin, and that I had to keep my word. At the time I thought Lynch believed it would be too difficult to get to Dublin, and, as an inspiration, the idea came to me if we sent a hundred men to Dublin to establish contact (and I had not the slightest doubt it could be easily done in the first two days) and when Lynch would see how easily it was done, I had hoped he would change his policy.

Liam Lynch agreed to let 100 men go, and he got Séumas Robinson to withdraw his resignation. He subsequently sent a Column from Tipperary to Dublin and they got as far as Blessington, about 15 miles south-west of Dublin. According to

Robinson the Column 'Did good work. I believe the "Staters" were almost as afraid of the Tipperary men coming to Dublin as if they were the Ghurkhas.'

The Battle of Dublin lasted from 28 June to 5 July. The Four Courts Garrison surrendered on 30 June. A tremendous explosion in the building destroyed the Public Records Office, and with it, centuries of historical paperwork. Many senior members of the IRA Executive were arrested.

Fighting continued in and around O'Connell Street for another few days after the fall of the Four Courts. Despite the outbreak of hostilities, many within the IRA still seemed reluctant to fully engage militarily. What Civil War entailed seemed too awful.

The Free State Army used artillery borrowed from the British. This was a decisive factor. Robinson was still adamant that the IRA should focus on Dublin; they outnumbered their enemy and should act decisively.

The prevailing tactic adopted by the IRA Divisions was to hold their areas. This developed into what Robinson described as 'line-fighting.' Despite disagreeing with the approach, Robinson ensured that his command area was fortified and he exploited the local geography.

The River Suir, with good roads on the north and south sides and a railway, all running parallel, was an ideal position for fighting on interior lines.

> With about five hundred rifles we held that line for weeks. It was never broken. The "Staters" passed on beyond us on both our flanks, wiped up the First Southern Division, and they were at Mitchelstown in our rear before the order was given to break up into Columns and harry the enemy with guerrilla tactics.

206

Robinson's command area kept the advance of the Free State forces at bay. It was crucial for him to hold out. It was recognised by Republicans that significant focus needed to be placed on the Second Southern Division area and it would emerge as the epicentre of resistance. Séumas Robinson established a Divisional Headquarters at Clonmel. One Volunteer stationed there, Phil Fitzgerald, remembered:

> As I crossed the barrack square very early one glorious July morning, I noticed a tall man, dressed in cap, trench coat and leggings, with a rifle slung loosely on his shoulder, talking to the sentry at the main gate. The sentry pointed in my direction. The "stranger" advanced towards me and asked if I could get him Séumas Robinson, Officer Commanding, Second Southern Division. I was happy to be able to comply immediately with his request - it was none other than Éamon de Valera. After the heat and strife and bitter disappointment of negotiations and debates, he had joined up as a private. Next day, Divisional Headquarters (to which I was now attached as Staff Officer) was shifted southwards to Carrick-on-Suir to be in closer touch with the fighting which had broken out in Waterford.

Robinson thought that the arrival of de Valera could have been a significant development and again the IRA should have reviewed its tactics.

> Mr. de Valera was with me (perhaps it would be better to say I was with him!) during the hottest part of the fighting, and had he had charge of the whole Army he would have turned the scales. But, the "have a bump off of them in your own area" style of Field General Headquarters would put the caip bháis on Napoleon himself.

Robinson felt constrained, especially since the Free State Army had changed their approach and landed by sea behind their lines. The dynamic had changed, but the IRA had nothing more imaginative in response other than resorting back to the guerrilla tactics deployed against the British, which would not work against former comrades. Robinson lamented:

After this the war was one of attrition, which at best could be indecisive only. Yet we held on, hoping against hope that someone in some other area, not so worn out as we were, would plead with the new Republican G.H.Q. and change our military policy. I am convinced that even two months after the break-up of our lines in August, had the Army been organised from Dublin in one last concerted attack on the enemy citadel - Dublin - we could have brought the war to a close, one way or other. That would have been more generous to the country, and probably we would have been successful. However, no use weeping over lost opportunities. I felt it would never be attempted - because Dublin was shell-shocked by the loss of the Four Courts and for the second time in six years Dublin was let down at a critical moment by the rest of the country.

The earlier steps undertaken by Robinson to prevent the Free State Army from seizing any barracks stood him in good stead. Parts of Tipperary remained as Republican strongholds but soon began to fall bit-by-bit under the advance of General Prout. The 'Munster Republic' began to crumble. It was to Robinson's command area that the other harried and harassed IRA Executive members retreated. Liam Lynch was eventually killed in the Knockmealdowns. Referring to this period, Robinson wrote:

Perhaps one of the most interesting things about this post line-fighting with us was the fact that we managed not only to establish a stationary permanent central Headquarters for the Division, but we even ran a weekly newspaper, "Chun an Lae," with Flora O'Keeffe as our Director of Publicity, from a fool-proof dugout at Maher's of Blackcastle. The weekly became known as "Tune and Lay." I wrote the first leading article to indicate our policy. After that it was in Flora's and Seán Fitzpatrick's hands.

Robinson realised that a counter-revolution was taking place. Emanating from societal elites, consisting of the Church, press, political, landed and business classes, Robinson sought to meet this challenge head on. He suppressed the Pro-Treaty Clonmel *Nationalist* newspaper and seized printing presses which were subsequently used for the Divisional paper, handbills, posters etc.

Robinson wanted to rally the ordinary people to the banner of the Irish Republic. In this period, his command area witnessed great social upheaval with workers creating cooperatives, land occupations and 'cattle drives.' The Red Flag flew in some areas. This didn't go down too well with his more conservative leaning comrades who maybe didn't appreciate the nature of their struggle and viewed it in purely military terms only.

Michael Hopkinson in his study of the Civil War highlighted that in one incident IRA members burned down one of the creameries in question. It was done for pure military reasons as they didn't want the advancing Free State Army to have a potential base in the area but it did result in the loss of support from the people of that particular locality. What is also interesting is that this action was done against Robinson's wishes. Without an overall coherent strategy and feeling the pressure of the Free State offensive, IRA discipline was all over the place.

Also notable in this period was Séumas Robinson's regard for female comrades. As recorded above, he appointed Flora

O'Keeffe to his Divisional Staff. Much later, during the military service pensions applications he acted as referee for many women whose roles may not have been recognised. In the case of Marian Tobin, he wrote a reference stating 'I personally have no hesitation in stating that, whether or not you were officially a member of CnamB [Cumann na mBan], you were de facto and de jure a member of the IRA.' Robinson writes that she received orders from IRA officers, and that even if she had been a member of Cumann na mBan, she would have immediately been seconded to his forces.

The Civil War turned increasingly vicious. Many notable leaders were killed, including Robinson's successor as Third Brigade OC, Dinny Lacey. On the Pro-Treaty, side Michael Collins died in controversial circumstances. Robinson had his own thoughts on that incident, believing Collins 'was bumped off' by someone within his own escort party. He recounted that Collins had been trying to make contact with Republicans as he was 'fed up with how things had developed. He had hoped that Republican elements within the Free State Government would be dominant but the O'Higgins-Cosgrave [faction] had got a grip...'

Collins was seeking some sort of concordat but many IRA leaders were suspicious and so nothing further seems to have developed. At the time of Collins's death, Robinson was in Dublin recuperating from a serious case of food poisoning, and so was unable to attend an IRA Executive meeting being held in Cork. Coincidentally, Collins was in Cork at the same time. Afterwards de Valera told Robinson that an IRA guard protecting the Executive meeting spotted a Free State convoy. They fired in order to alert the Executive. Robinson relates:

> Naturally they fired in the direction of the cars. The guards had to retreat immediately. Now, if the few shots fired in the direction of the cars half a mile away could have picked

out Michael Collins and shot him in the back of the head then it surely was providential! But people who saw the corpse say that the hair on the back of the head was singed!

Robinson further believed that the secretive nature of the inquest was highly suspicious and nothing was revealed. He asked 'Did the ex-British element do Collins in to prevent him from getting in touch with the IRA?'

Executions, internment, hunger strikes, reprisals and the destruction of infrastructure crippled the country at large. The IRA was very much on-the-run by the spring of 1923. After the death of Lynch, the only logical step to take was to dump arms and call a ceasefire. Military defeat was the conclusion. Many IRA leaders ended up in prison or were hunted night and day.

For Séumas Robinson, he was a broken man. His dream, his vision, his goal, everything he worked for was 'torn up for bandages.' The Republic was lost. Having endured many hardships over the last several years, from the Easter Rising to imprisonment, infrequent meals and sleep, cold damp conditions, living on-the-run and the constant danger eventually took its toll. His health completely broke down, and he escaped Ireland and travelled incognito to the Isle of Man in order to recuperate. Returning to Ireland, he avoided capture until the General Amnesty of June 1924. Séumas Robinson and Peadar O'Donnell, who had escaped from prison, were the first Republican leaders to emerge from hiding and walked the streets of Dublin to test the bona fides of the amnesty.

Republicans seemed defeated. Politically, they were moribund. Séumas Robinson continued as a member of the Second Dáil, viewed by Republicans as the legitimate parliament of the Irish Republic. While contesting Free State elections they would not contemplate taking their seats due to the Oath of Allegiance.

They were isolated and many within their ranks felt that this could not continue indefinitely. People like Robinson and Seán McEntee, who both had northern roots, were fearful that partition would remain a permanent feature if Republicans could not gain political power. Robinson referred to the political entity in the 26 counties as 'a wee mutilated state.'

Éamon de Valera began to articulate the position that if the oath could be surmounted then they should take their seats. This was anathema to many within Sinn Féin, and so de Valera broke away and formed a new political party: Fianna Fáil. This 'new departure' had the tacit consent of many within the Republican Movement and numbered amongst its founders was Séumas Robinson. He was suspicious of politics and politicians but realised that, militarily, their struggle was over and that they needed political power to advance their cause. He, nevertheless, had a very close relationship with de Valera that had developed during the Civil War and was prepared to invest in the proposed political project.

Robinson was elected to Seanad Éireann in 1928 as part of a small contingent led by fellow Belfastman, Joe Connolly. In the Seanad, Robinson articulated their position:

> Republicans say they will never Crown anyone King of Ireland... We are neither Pro-Treaty or Anti-Treaty – we just don't bother about it; it does not matter... we will make use of the Treaty so long as it's in existence. The Treaty does not worry us one way or the other. What does worry us is getting absolute freedom.

Despite his consent and participation in this new political venture, Séumas Robinson never seemed at ease. He appeared to be a reluctant politician and resigned his seat before his term concluded, in December 1934. The following year he was appointed a member of the Military Service Pension Board which validated claims for service during the years of insurgency. Robinson went out of his way to ensure genuine claimants received what they deserved. It was an extremely bureaucratic process, and the recently released files are peppered with references from him. Indeed, he even had difficulty in getting claims for himself validated, and didn't show up for what he thought was a demeaning medical examination. His brother Joe also had difficulties as did his wife Brigid, who felt that she was further penalised due to Séumas's membership of the board, as he could not be called as a witness or referee on her behalf. Next, Robinson was appointed to the Military History Bureau, and so he spent much of his later career compiling stories from participants in the struggle for Irish Freedom – the struggle to which he devoted his life.

POSTSCRIPT

Hopefully this small portrait of a revolutionary has demonstrated that although a marginalised figure, Séumas Robinson played a pivotal and at times crucial part during the campaign for Irish Independence from 1916 – 1923. History has not been kind to Robinson. He has been overlooked in favour of some South Tipperary locals. Robinson referred to this as 'The Great Tipperary Hoax' and, apart from a few perfunctory attempts, he never made a sustained effort to counter this narrative in the public arena. He knew, as did people who played a role in the struggle, who did what, where and when. In later life, he would not associate himself with commemorations, events or publications which he felt were promoting this 'hoax.' As OC of the Brigade, he believed that he — and he alone — was an authority on the overall struggle in South Tipperary. He outlined this position to newspaper editors, who would not print his rebuttals, and to the Soloheadbeg Commemoration Committee. He refused to attend the official unveiling of a monument in January 1950. Writing to the Committee to decline his invitation Robinson stated:

> I have never yet tried to sound my own horn, nor have I ever yet attempted to wash dirty linen in public - I have never even complained in public - because I had hoped (forlornly?) that some generous-minded Tipperary man would someday try to redeem what other Tipperary men have done (or left undone) to a stranger who went amongst them out of love for Ireland to do a certain job for Ireland and Tipperary and who did it. Until that is done, I will continue to feel that, had I served my country in any other

214

part of Ireland as I have served her in South Tipperary, I would not have been damned with slight praise and worse, for the last thirty years. I am sure that you will now appreciate properly why I cannot with any semblance of self-respect, accept your Committee's invitation – or any other similar invitation from South Tipperary.

A major source of contention for Robinson in the narrative of the period focused upon Dan Breen's *My Fight for Irish Freedom*. This book was the first account to enter the public domain, published towards the end of 1924. The Civil War was literally only over, Republicans were defeated with many still held in camps and prisons. The rawness of that embittered struggle was more than fresh. The book was ghost-written by Kitty O'Doherty from notes she received from Breen. Entertaining in the style of a Western, it proved to be very popular as it dealt, in that first edition, exclusively with the fight against the British. It was, nevertheless, a self-aggrandising version of events, claiming personal responsibility for everything that happened in Tipperary during the War for Independence. Robinson took exception to it on several fronts including Breen's claims around rank and leadership as well as participation in elements of the fight where he was not present. Robinson dismissed it as a work of fiction, stating that he preferred 'Buck Rogers.' Under scrutiny, many of the claims in the book do not stand up. Other written accounts, such as Ernie O'Malley's in reference to the barracks attacks, do not validate Breen's version. It seems he was in Dublin for much of the period. New material that has emerged from the Bureau of Military Witness Statements or Pension Submissions again contradict much of what Breen claimed. Breen's version was the first account put forward and so by merit of being first became synonymous with events in Tipperary. Although it appeared to be common knowledge about the veracity of Breen's account, it remained unchallenged and was to remain a source of personal

215

hurt to Robinson. Indeed, Breen does not repeat many of the claims in his Witness Statement. In an often contradictory narrative he instead promotes that a premeditated process of intrigue to exert behind the scenes command of the Brigade was hatched between himself and Treacy, thus diminishing Robinson's role to that of a nominal leader. Obviously Seán Treacy could not verify these claims. Without doubt, Robinson did have issues exerting full control, that's the nature of guerilla warfare; it comes with the territory and leadership is a lonely post. The rift between the two former comrades would never be healed. Robinson was further vexed with what he saw as Breen's maverick behaviour before the commencement of and during the Civil War, for entering the Free State Dáil before it was official Fianna Fáil policy and for — as Robinson alleged — accepting a pension and renumeration for medical bills from the Free State Government. Séumas Robinson would never escape from the 'hoax.' It even extended to his obituary in the *Irish Press*, which stated that he was 'with' Breen at Soloheadbeg. This animosity would re-emerge posthumously with their Witness Statements to the Military History Bureau, with each outlining their respective viewpoints.

Despite not receiving proper credit, Robinson was a key architect of the guerrilla struggle that emerged from 1919. Drawing upon his experiences of Easter Week 'where I got a training … [that] enabled me to formulate the plan – shoot them out when you can, burn them out when you can't and be out when they expect to find you in.' It was recognised by those around him that he brought a new dynamic to Tipperary. He was sincere, dedicated, brave and would lead from the front. Twice promoted in the field during Easter Week from Volunteer to Section Leader then to First Lieutenant, his experiences throughout that episode would influence him for the rest of his life. He was the only elected Brigadier of South Tipperary during this period; his successor, Dinny Lacey, was appointed.

Robinson was given Divisional Command, elected to both the IRA Army Executive and Army Council and was tasked with assisting in the fortification of Dublin during the Treaty Crisis, all of which demonstrates the faith and confidence placed in him by his comrades. He had a singular focus and possessed a determination to fight for the cause of Irish Freedom no matter where it took him. Indeed, coming to Tipperary in the first instance highlights that. It would have been a completely alien environment for someone who originated from the industrial cities of Belfast and Glasgow. The endemic poverty, cramped conditions and sectarianism were a world apart from the lush, spacious and fertile valleys of rural Tipperary.

Séumas Robinson was instrumental in ensuring that armed struggle began. Soloheadbeg was intended primarily to capture explosives. There was no prior intent to kill, but there was a willingness to use their weapons if needed. Soloheadbeg helped put military action back on the agenda, given the pre-eminence of the political struggle in the wake of the successful results in the 1918 election and the formation of the Dáil. The reaction to Soloheadbeg demonstrated that not everyone was in the frame of mind to accept fully the needs and consequences of a conflict that this action presaged. Soloheadbeg had a quality of stark reality which braced the Volunteer mind for the task looming ahead.

The merit of Soloheadbeg was that it was the 'premier coup,' but the 'follow through' came with the rescue of Seán Hogan at Knocklong. This was the first time that known and wanted men had carried out such a daring deed. The 'Knocklong effect' would be far reaching. Robinson described that 'The Army was like a network of explosive mines and we were the battery that set off the first explosion in the chain of explosions all over Ireland that blasted the way to the Truce.' However, there is a valid criticism focusing on the absence of the Brigade leadership

217

from the locality for much of the period after Knocklong. When Robinson and Treacy returned to the area, things began to happen with more vigour.

The reaction from Dublin to their actions in South Tipperary would ensure that the future relationship between Robinson, GHQ and indeed even the Dáil would be one consisting of mutual distrust and suspicion. He had a hatred of 'Red Tape' and refused to furnish GHQ with written reports on Brigade activity after files were caught at a GHQ office located in Cullenswood House, which resulted in major raids across his Command Area. GHQ and their bureaucracy were a distraction for Robinson; in fact, he thought they were a hindrance to his notion of 'autonomous freelancers.'

The Treaty derailed the years of unison. Some within the ranks of the Republican Movement were prepared to accept compromise; others were not. The legacy of Civil War was to blight Ireland for years. The 'terrible beauty born in 1916 had lost its good looks' when brother began killing brother. Tactically the IRA blundered; internal divisions and localism were exploited by the Free State forces. Robinson, in vain, tried to shift IRA attitudes, but it never happened and they ended up broken and defeated. Something he would never get over.

In later years, he would hark back to the glorious years of unity from 1916 -1921. He would maintain close ties with members of the Scottish IRA and 'Kimmage Garrison.' His work with the Pension Bureau and Military History Bureau would bring him into contact with people involved with the struggle from all parts of Ireland. He would have the honour of leading many Easter Commemorations in Dublin, but his relationship with Tipperary would never be fixed.

A loving family man, he and his wife Brigid, along with their children, resided in Dublin. For those close to him it was noticed that a great serenity descended on Robinson in his later years. It was almost like he had retreated, in his mind, back to the solitude and tranquillity of the Monastery. He was very much at ease with the part he had played and was prepared to defend the ethics and morality of their actions. He did this in regards to Soloheadbeg in a letter to the press under the pseudonym of 'Dalariada', the ancient Gaelic Kingdom of Western Scotland and North Eastern Ireland. Being a civil servant, he could not put his name to it but was no less determined to ensure accusations of impropriety were countered.

Séumas Robinson died a few years after his wife on 8 December 1961. Oscar Traynor, in his funeral oration expressed the desire that Séumas Robinson would not be written out of history. Reading between the lines, Traynor was very much conscious about the process that had side-lined Robinson and it seems he felt that it was wrong, as did many others but they never spoke out. Breen was local; he was a Fianna Fáil TD and so the dirty linen would certainly not be aired in public. A grave injustice was perpetrated against Robinson, one that the passage of time has not really fixed. It is only now that his commanding and pivotal role has been brought together in the pages of this publication, tracing his extraordinary journey from Sevastopol Street in Belfast to Soloheadbeg and the events that have shaped modern Ireland.

Appendices

The Third Tipperary Brigade IRA Structure (From: *With the IRA in The Fight for Freedom – The Red Path of Glory*). *Published by the Kerryman 1950*

The Third (or South) Tipperary Brigade had for its field of operations the southern portion of the county, an area stretching from the western end of the Glen of Aherlow to the boundary of county Waterford on the south and extending sides to Tipperary, Hollyford, Rossmore, Dualla, Killenaule and Drangan.

Séumas Robinson OC

Conn Ó Maoldomhnaigh Adjutant (Acting for Maurice Crowe)

First Battalion (Tipperary)
(1). Seán Duffy (2). Con Moloney (3). Tom Ryan (4). Denis Lacy

Second Battalion (Dundrum)
(1). T Dwyer (2). M Sheehan (3). Phil Fitzgerald (4). Jack Ryan (Laurence)

Third Battalion (Cashel)
(1). Séamus Ó Néill (2). J Gorman (3). P Hogan (4). Pat Casey

Fourth Battalion (Clonmel)
(1). Frank Drohan (2) Bill Myles (3). William Hanrahan (4). Séamus Kennedy

Fifth Battalion (Cahir)
(1). _ McGrath (2). Michael Ledrigan (3). Bill Casey

Sixth Battalion (Drangan)
(1). T Donovan

Seventh Battalion (Carrick-on-Suir)
(1). John O'Keeffe

Eighth Battalion (Rosegreen)
(1). J Davin (2). P Quinn (3). J Delahunty (4). J Purcell

Excerpts from Treaty Debates in Dáil Éireann

Private Session 17 December 1921

MR. SÉUMAS ROBINSON: Another vexed question raised by Mr. Hogan was the Oath. A great many clever men seem to think it is not an oath and others seem to think it is because Lloyd George himself seems to think it is. I am a Republican and I hope there remain Republicans, so many great men have changed I fear for myself too. Touching on the different documents, certainly I am not in love with Tweedledum or Tweedledee but still I believe there is a difference but it is not a difference worth fighting about. Now some Deputies have said that allowing these men to go to London was sufficient guarantee on our part that we were prepared for a certain amount of compromise. I deny that the words "associate with" can mean absolutely nothing that they are associations as France could be with England. We are not tying ourselves in any way and I think the President made that clear in his speech. I also used to think that Lloyd George had bluffed this country. I think the President is really the man who started this association idea in the country. It is not a matter of killing soldiers at all. This is not a war similar to the one that England was waging against Germany. She could and should round up every German in the country. England could not do that with Irishmen at all and Irishmen would always be there. That is the peculiar difference, I think. All this talk about English extermination we have heard ever since we were youngsters. I say that 50 men in England would be able to counteract any destruction that the British could do because thanks to British oppression we are not a manufacturing country like England and if she destroyed every home in Ireland, I believe in 5 years we could rebuild. England depends upon her factories and shipyards and we could work more destruction in England than she could on us. At any rate, it would be a permanent loss to England and it would be only a temporary loss to us. We are not going to fight the whole British nation. Fifty men across in England could do more damage than any serious fighting.

Public Session 6 January 1922

MR. SÉUMAS ROBINSON: In my own plain, direct, if not too lucid way, I would like to fire a few shots at this Treaty—metaphorically speaking. To begin with, it seems to me that the Republic is at stake. Ratifiers should remember that we poor, benighted Republicans have not yet seen the light. They themselves did not see the light two months ago. If we lose our tempers a bit and think terrible things of them it should be charitably remembered that the ratifiers have changed, and it is their duty to listen patiently to us and then try to answer our questions. The Deputy for Clontarf, Deputy Mulcahy, sees no alternative. It is the Republic. The Republic is at stake and I don't care a rap whose reputation is torn up for bandages. This is the same man who often before declared to me that there was no danger of compromise. To my mind this compromise has been lurking in the ante-camera of many a cerebrum for the past three years. It was conceived when the Volunteers were denied a general convention three years ago; it passed through the embryo form when the Volunteers began to be controlled solely from Dublin Headquarters; it became a chrysalis when Dublin H.Q. became a wage-earning business, when District H.Q. were set up by General H.Q. and paid to control men who fought the war, aye, and won it, without any appreciable assistance from Dublin Headquarters. One division in the South refused this money and they were told that it would be made a point of discipline if they did not accept. On the night prior to the Tuesday morning on which the Treaty was announced in the papers, the Chief of Staff laughed at me for again expressing to him and the Military Officer in Limerick, the fear that all these mysterious goings-on in London foreboded nothing but compromise—for truth and straight-dealing flourish in the light. Yes! Now we have got our beautiful compromises hatched out— just like all compromises, like the mule—it is barren. Our Chief Officer stated, and the Minister for Finance and others maintained, that the acceptance of this [289] invitation amounted to an attempt at compromise. All I would say about that is this: that we trusted him, and it is hardly fair for him to blame us for trusting him. Now, the appeal to humanity is: are we going to give our moral or immoral support to England in her efforts to crush Egypt and India, which countries have given us the sincerest form of flattery by imitating us? For my part I would give no support to any attempt at association with England, either politically or economically, while she is suppressing with brute force any people—much less such splendid peoples as the Hindus and Egyptians. Men who call ideals and symbols shadows and unrealities are, to my mind, defective human beings. I would ask the Irish people—yes, and the English people, too—for our quarrel is with the few English ruling families only —I would ask these peoples can you ever again trust these men, shall you trust them now? I will say this to the English people: do you not think that if you wish an honourable world peace, it would be better for you, for us, and for humanity as a whole that you fix up a humane peace—if I may put it like that —with all your present subject peoples. Why not call a conference of these peoples and the British peoples and hammer out an entente cordiale—a workable confederation of sovereign states into which other nations could be invited if we saw fit. I think there are great possibilities in that suggestion and I wonder it has not been suggested by someone who could attract attention. What I am going to say now may appear on the surface to be a contradiction of what I have just suggested—I wish to state emphatically that no people have the right to go into any empire, much less an Empire that is based on a big section of downtrodden humanity. They have no right because it would mean slavery of some type; and no form of slavery is a fit state for free-willed human beings; therefore, if we are in the minority of one, there will be one to fight against it. I wish to state that this Treaty does not mean peace; and I think that should be fairly obvious by this time. Chaos would be better by far than degradation. It may not seem to be degradation to many people, but it does seem so to some and these some may not have it. Those who are breaking away can come back; we cannot change, we who regard ideals and symbols as something worthwhile. I say that chaos can be avoided and peace will be at least possible if those who have changed return to the Republic; if not we will have chaos and war. This paper which I will now read for you will prove the serious view that thousands of Volunteers take of this thing that appears to be a betrayal. It is a copy of a letter received by me to-day. Here it is: "In view of the false rumours that have been circulated about Dublin to the effect that we, the undersigned, have declared ourselves favourable to the acceptance of the proposed Treaty of Agreement between the Irish plenipotentiaries and those of Great Britain, we desire, first, to enter our emphatic protest against the use of our Division of the Army to influence public opinion and the opinion of members of Dáil Eireann in the direction favourable to the Treaty; and we desire, secondly, to state that we maintain unimpaircd our allegiance to the Irish Republic and to it alone. The Divisions comprise the following Brigades: 1st Southern Division: Cork, Nos. 1, 2, 3, 4, 5 Brigade. Kerry, Nos. 1, 2, 3 Brigade; West Limerick Brigade; Waterford Brigade. Dublin Brigade. 3rd Southern Division: Tipperary No. 1 Brigade; Offaly No. 2 Brigade; Leix Brigade. Signed on behalf of the above-mentioned Divisions and Brigades, Liam Lynch, O.C. 1st Southern Division; Earnán Ó Máille, O.C. 2nd Southern

Division; Oscar Traynor, O.C. Dublin Brigade; Micheál MacCormaic, O.C. 3rd Southern Division."

MR. ROBINSON: The army has always been regarded as the army pure and simple. I submit that it is not so. If we had no political outlook, we would not be soldiers at all.

PRESIDENT DE VALERA: I know that they are citizen-soldiers. The point is that bringing them up as Brigades is not wise.

MR. ROBINSON: I think the Volunteers have been very badly treated. The Volunteers demand a veto on the change of our country's constitution. We are not a national army in the ordinary sense; we are not a machine pure and simple; we have political views as soldiers. For the purpose of this veto I here demand a general convention of the Volunteers who are not Truce Volunteers. The Volunteers never gave up their right to a general convention— the Oath of Allegiance in this weak, in this changeable Dáil was not sanctioned by the general convention. If this convention is granted I, with I am sure all Volunteers, would refrain from certain terrible action that will be necessary if the Treaty is forced on us without our consent as an Army of Volunteers. There is no fear of the outcome of a renewal of war.

MR. MILROY: Gambling again.

MR. ROBINSON: Our war is not a war between two ordinary nations such as England and Germany; England had no German subjects. Our position is unique; we can, and will if necessary, strike the Empire where and how no other people could do it— except the Scotch and Welsh if they should so choose. The English ruling families know this well; one of their delegates declared our war to be a peculiar war— enough said! We are not a definite objective to the British, while they will always be a

226

vulnerable objective to the Irish Empire, because one thousand effective shots and one thousand effective fires in Britain would ruin England for ever; while we could recover any damage in five years—we have no debt and no great factories, comparatively speaking and their destruction would mean comparatively little to us. We could fight the English for three years—the English themselves could not fight us for longer than six months, especially if we took the fight up seriously in England as well as in Ireland and India and Egypt. Perhaps we will be told again and again that we would be exterminated. There will always be ten Irishmen who will even up matters someday, should it be ninety years hence. Dr. White says England would lose India and Egypt and England itself—every man—rather than lose Ireland. Does the doctor, does not every Irishman care as much about Ireland as the English do? Irishmen, are you working for your country? There are many people in the Dáil and in the country and all over the world, who cannot understand big questions of such complication as this Treaty, and haven't time to form an opinion, and who, naturally, will form their opinion on, or rather take their opinion from, their pet hero. There are many thousand people enthusiastic supporters of the Treaty simply because Michael Collins is its mother—possibly Arthur Griffith would be called its father. Now, it is only natural and right that many people should follow almost blindly a great and good man. But suppose you know that such a man was not really such a great man; and that his reputation and great deeds of daring were in existence only on paper and in the imagination of people who read stories about him. If Michael Collins is the great man he is supposed to be, he has a right to influence people and people ought to be influenced by him. Now Dr. MacCartan said that he could understand many people saying: "What is good enough for Michael Collins is good enough for me." Arthur Griffith has called Collins "the man who won the war." The Press has called him the Commander-in-Chief of the I.R.A. He has been called "a great exponent of guerrilla warfare" and the "elusive Mike" and we have all read the story of the White Horse. There are stories going round Dublin of fights he had all over the city—the Custom House in particular. If Michael Collins was all that he has been called then I will admire him and respect his opinions, if my little mind cannot comprehend his present attitude towards the Republic and this Treaty. Now, from my knowledge of character and psychology, which I'm conceited enough to think is not too bad, I'm forced to think that the reported Michael Collins could not possibly be the same Michael Collins who was so weak as to compromise the Republic.

MR. KEVIN O'HIGGINS: On a point of order. Are we discussing Michael Collins or the Treaty?

A DEPUTY: Or are we impeaching him?

MR. ROBINSON: The weak man who signed certainly exists and just as certainly therefore, I believe the reported Michael Collins did not ever exist. If Michael Collins who signed the Treaty ever did the wonderful things reported of him then I'm another fool. But before I finally admit myself a fool, I want some authoritative statement. I want, and I think it all important that the Dáil, the country, aye, and the world, got authoritative answers to the following questions: (a) What positions exactly did Michael Collins hold in the Army? (b) Did he ever take part in any armed conflict in which he fought by shooting; the number of such battles or fights; in fact, is there any authoritative record of his having ever fired a shot for Ireland at an enemy of Ireland?

MR. GAVAN DUFFY: Is this in order?

THE SPEAKER: I don't want to interrupt but I think it is as near not discussing the Treaty as possible.

MR. ROBINSON: Now, so far as I know, Michael Collins came over from London as I came from Glasgow to avoid Conscription.

MR. BLYTHE: That's not true.

MR. ROBINSON: And to fight for Ireland instead of for England; and if Michael Collins says—and he has said it here—that the fight that we have been waging for two-and-a-half years is an impossible war, well it gives me furiously to think—bluff, coercion, duress, treachery and the lot. Somebody used the word "impeach"—well, that is true. Delegates are in the dock to some extent at least; they have done something that at first sight, at least, appears to be—well, treason. I maintain that they have been guilty of the act of high treason and betrayal; I believe they were guilty deliberately but not maliciously. In fairness to themselves they must clear themselves for they will be judged through all the coming years. I'll try to confine myself to facts and obvious points mostly. I will try to draw a few fair inferences: (1) Remember Lloyd George is a past master in political stage craft. (2) Remember Wilson and the London atmosphere. (3) Remember Arthur Griffith could hardly be bluffed nor Michael Collins. Arthur Griffith is a match for Lloyd George and Lloyd George is a match for Arthur Griffith. (4) Remember when these two men came together it is possible that they both soon realised that if they fought neither would win; and they realised also that there might be a way in which they could both win a victory over their respective Cabinets. (5) There is clear proof that two delegates signed under duress and that two delegates and one say that there was no duress. (6) Arthur Griffith and Michael Collins declared they really did not sign under duress though they speak of the time limit and the threat of terrible and immediate war. By the way, let us take Arthur Griffith and Michael Collins at their word and believe they were not forced to sign; then they must have done this with, shall I say, malice aforethought; and must have aided by their signatures and demeanour to bluff and stampede the rest of the delegation into signing too—that is how the matter strikes me, anyhow. Arthur Griffith declares he would not break on the Crown. I suggest Lloyd George knew this, too; and our Cabinet knew it; and in order to safeguard themselves and the Republic they gave the delegates instructions not to sign any final draft before submitting it to the Cabinet. Remember that Lloyd George probably knew—must have known—that the Republican Government would have rejected the Treaty as it stands had it come unsigned. Remember Arthur Griffith would not like to lose the child of former dreams of his life's labour, more especially when, as far as he could see, there was no chance of getting his newer step-son or foster-child—the Republic. I submit Lloyd George knew this, too; and that he probably saw—I'd say he did see—the possibility of satisfying Arthur Griffith and of making himself appear the greatest of British statesmen in eight hundred years by giving us Dominion Home Rule. Would it be too much to say that these two men came to an agreement to force, gently, this Treaty, down the necks of their respective Cabinets—with Michael Collins a willing backer the thing would not seem too difficult. Remember, Lloyd George and Arthur Griffith and Michael Collins had meetings at which the other delegates were not present. Remember that now these men—Arthur Griffith and Michael Collins—declare that they want substance, that they are not idealists; could they not have been of the same mind before, that is, previous to signing the Treaty? Remember that if Lloyd George, Arthur Griffith and Michael Collins thought that if they had a right to put their scheme on their respective countries— after all they could say and justly so: "We know this is the only, and therefore the best way Irish co-operation can be reconciled with the British Commonwealth of Nations" —they would know also that it would not be a success unless it could be bluffed on us and slipped on us; and would require very careful handling and a judicious amount of realistic stage play —a chance for Lloyd George here. Hence I submit this is the origin of the time limit, the immediate and terrible war threat, the appearance of armed auxiliaries rushing around Dublin and the making of camps all over Ireland just previous to the time for signing the Treaty. Look here, all this was not arranged in a couple of hours. Remember that negotiations were going on for eight weeks, was it. All the talks must surely have been on details only, they must have been leaving essentials, i.e., the oath and status to the end. It seems a strange way of doing business, and I'm afraid the Cabinet as a whole are not altogether without blame for this. Again, I submit that to recommend their scheme of Dominion Home Rule effectively to the country they would naturally fix up details first. A decision on essentials too soon would be disastrous—at least a decision on essentials would be disastrous if it were known too soon. Then, when all would be ready, a time limit and an immediate war stunt could be requisitioned to carry the remaining members off their feet. Remember, they were carried off their feet by this, coupled with the sight of the signatures of the two formidable men of the delegation. What is good enough for Michael Collins is good enough for me—what is a terror to Michael Collins ought to be a terror enough for me. Finally, above all things considered, there is a prima facie case, I think, for the charge of treason against the delegates, Arthur Griffith and Michael Collins. No doubt they will give a satisfactory explanation of their efforts; and I would be more than delighted to withdraw any imputation that my words may unjustly convey. I think they should thank me for saying openly what is in the minds of many. They will have a chance to-morrow to answer this.

Members of the Army Unity Committee 1922

Pro-Treaty: Michael Collins, Richard Mulcahy, Diarmuid O'Hegarty, Eoin O'Duffy, Gearóid O'Sullivan and Seán MacEoin.

Anti-Treaty: Liam Lynch, Liam Mellows, Seán Moylan, Séumas Robinson and Rory O'Connor.

IRA Army Executive elected 9 April 1922

Liam Lynch, Liam Mellows, Rory O'Connor, Joe McKelvey, Florence O'Donaghue, Sean Moylan, Seán O'Hegarty, Liam Deasy, Séumas Robinson, Ernie O'Malley, Peadar O'Donnell, Joe O'Connor, Frank Barrett, Tom Maguire, PJ Ruttledge and Tom Hales.

Army Council elected 9 April 1922

Liam Lynch (Chief of Staff), Rory O'Connor, Liam Mellows, Joe McKelvey, Ernie O'Malley, Séumas Robinson and Peadar O'Donnell.

Army Executive 28 June 1922

Liam Lynch, Liam Deasy, Rory O'Connor, Liam Mellows, Joe McKelvey, Peadar O'Donnell, Tom Derrig, Ernie O'Malley, Tom Barry, Michael Kilroy, PJ Ruttledge, Frank Barrett, Pax Whelan, Seán Moylan, Séumas Robinson and Joe O'Connor

Co-options for those captured: Seán Lehane for Peadar O'Donnell. Frank Aiken for Joe McKelvey. Seán McSwiney for Liam Mellows. Con Moloney for Rory O'Connor.

Letter written by Séumas Robinson to the Irish Times around the ethics of the Soloheadbeg Ambush:

Soloheadbeg

Sir – Surely the "letters to the editor" column of a newspaper is not an appropriate place to initiate a debate, with each correspondent flying off at his own pet tangents, on the ethics of Soloheadbeg ambush, or say on the morality of French partisans shooting down German soldiers "going about their peaceful duties" after the official surrender of France; or again, on the morality or immorality, in the light of international decency, not to say Christian theology, of Irishmen joining the British Army and killing people who were fighting for their own countries?

What do some of your correspondents hope to achieve? Do they want to show (with secret delight?) that the British Empire – excuse me – that this wee mutilated State of ours was conceived and brought forth in iniquity and must come to a bad end (their "bad end" justifying their means?). However, at least one of your correspondents, a lady, seems to be genuinely worried; perhaps the following relevant points may help:

(1) The existence of the first Dáil had not yet been promulgated throughout the country when the ambush took place.

(2) The men at Soloheadbeg ambush acted under standing

directions of the Army to obtain arms and munitions when and where they could be got. Virtually tons of explosives had been captured in Scotland by the Fianna and I.R.B. and sent to Dublin for the 1916 Rising, and at least one big raid was carried out in Dublin before Easter Week. These raids for munitions were a well-established routine.

(3) That the two unfortunate and brave R.I.C. men refused to surrender is abundantly clear to anyone who read the evidence of the inquest and remembers it. What is not so clear is that the policemen tried to shoot after they were called on two or three times to surrender.

(4) – Oh! What's the use! The more light you show to a bigot, the more he shuts it out, like the pupil of a cat's eye. – Yours, etc.

"Dalariada"
Dublin, February 6th, 1950.

The Irish Press, 9 December 1961

Death of Séumas Robinson

The death occurred in Dublin last night of Commandant-General Séumas Robinson, former O.C. of the Second Southern Division IRA and one of the most outstanding figures in the fight for freedom.

He took part in the 1916 Rising in Dublin and was with Dan Breen at Soloheadbeg and at Knocklong, and in the attack on Lord French at Ashtown.

When the Civil War started, Commandant-General Robinson, who had been elected as one of the 16 members of the Executive of the Volunteers, decided to carry on the war against the British. He was a former member of Dáil Éireann having been elected for East Tipperary and Waterford in 1921. After the Civil War he joined Fianna Fáil and was elected a Senator in 1928.

Séumas Robinson was the ideal Citizen Soldier. He came to the fight for Irish Freedom via Belfast and Glasgow because he realised that such a step was necessary. He explained his attitude during the Treaty Debates when he was a member of the Second Dáil. He declared:

"The Army has always been regarded as the army pure and simple. I submit this is not so. If we had no political outlook, we would not be soldiers at all… we are not the national army in an ordinary sense: we are not a machine pure and simple; we have political views as soldiers."

He was speaking then as a senior officer of the Army as well as a member of the Dáil.

Born in Belfast

Séumas Robinson was born in Belfast in 1890 and got his early education at the CBS there and at various parts of Scotland. He was part of the Scottish contingent of Volunteers which came for the Rising of 1916. He joined the organisation in 1913 at its inception.

He had one of the most dangerous tasks in Easter Week being in charge of a small outpost in O'Connell Street at Hopkins and Hopkins shop. Later he shared in the common fate of survivors and went in to prison in Britain.

Soon after his release he was one of those imprisoned in Belfast Jail at the time of the big prison revolt led by Austin Stack.

While he was on his way to Dublin from Belfast after his release, he was told by Michael Collins that he had been elected Brigade O.C. of the Third Tipperary Brigade. Seán Treacy had turned down the appointment in favour of Robinson. That was in June 1918.

It was Séumas Robinson's men that had carried out the attack at Soloheadbeg and Knocklong and many other attacks on the enemy in their area. He came with Breen and Treacy and others to take part in the attack on Lord French at Ashtown.

Those were the dark days of 1920, the year that saw Treacy's death and Breen's fight in Drumcondra.

At the time of his election to the Dáil Séumas Robinson was Brigade Commandant of the Third Tipperary Brigade and was put forward because Collins wanted as many active Volunteers and possible in the Dáil.

Commandant General Robinson's death occurred at Mount Carmel Nursing Home, Dublin. His remains will be removed this evening at 5.30pm to the Church of the Three Patrons, where the funeral will take place to Glasnevin after 9 O'Clock Mass on Monday.